Ye Oldest Diarie Of Englysshe Travell: Being The Hitherto Unpublished Narrative Of The Pilgrimage Of Sir Richard Torkington To Jerusalem In 1517...

Richard Torkington

Ƿe Oldeſt Diarie of Englyſſhe Travell:

BEING THE HITHERTO UNPUBLISHED NARRATIVE
OF THE PILGRIMAGE OF SIR RICHARD TORKINGTON
TO JERUSALEM IN 1517.

[ONE SHILLING.]

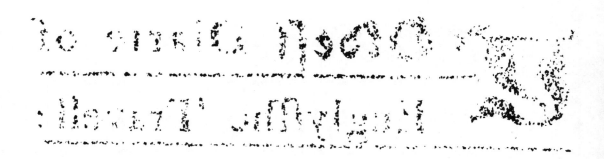

No. vi.

The
Vellum-Parchment Shilling Series

or

Miscellaneous Literature.

Field & Tuer,
Ye Leadenhalle Presse, E.C.

Torkington's Pilgrimage.

Ye Oldest Diarie of Englysshe Travell:

BEING THE HITHERTO UNPUBLISHED NARRATIVE
OF THE PILGRIMAGE OF SIR RICHARD TORKINGTON
TO JERUSALEM IN 1517.

EDITED BY W. J. LOFTIE,

B.A., F.S.A., Author of "A History of London," &c., &c.

———

LONDON :

FIELD & TUER, Ye LEADENHALLE PRESSE, E.C.

SIMPKIN, MARSHALL & Co.   HAMILTON, ADAMS & Co.

[COPYRIGHT

LONDON :

FIELD & TUER

YE LEADENHALLE PRESSE, E.C.

T 3,216.

A Short Account of Torkington's Pilgrimage.

 LTHOUGH Sir John Maundevile's travels were made more than a century before the pilgrimage of Sir Richard Torkington, no apology is necessary for calling attention to a veritable diary in which the author's personal adventures are the principal subject. Of Sir Richard we only know that he was

a priest, and that he was presented in 1511 to the rectory of Mulberton, in Norfolk, by Sir Thomas Boleyn, afterwards Earl of Wiltshire, the father of Henry the Eighth's ill-fated second wife.

The two manuscripts of Torkington's diary, which exist in the British Museum, are both copies. The older one must be very nearly contemporary with the parson of Mulberton himself; but the other was made in the last century by an antiquary named Wheler, who resided in the classic region of Stratford-upon-Avon.* On a loose leaf inserted into this copy are some notes on difficulties in the text by Wheler himself, and by another writer; but

---

* Mr. Wheler described the diary in an article published in the *Gentleman's Magazine*, in October, 1812. The old MS. and Wheler's copy are now in the British Museum: Addl. MSS. 28,561 and 28,562.

they do not on the whole throw much light on the subject. Most of the points which puzzled them are due to the carelessness of the first copier, and would no doubt be easily cleared up if Torkington's own manuscript should ever be found. For example "somer castyll" occurs in a passage which shows that the copier misread "fower castle," for Torkington evidently means the forecastle or "fo'castle" of a ship. So, too, in another place, where Torkington must have written "calys," meaning "chalice," his copier has turned the c into b, and Mr. Wheler appears to have thought a scourge or besom was intended, connecting "balys" with the French *balais*.* On the whole, however, the manuscript is very easily read, and the general meaning plain, in spite of a method, or rather the want of a method,

---

* See under "Baleys" in Way's *Promptorium Parvulorum*, p. 22.

of spelling which is only rivalled in Leland's *Itinerary*, a very nearly contemporary work.

Torkington started on his pilgrimage on the Friday before mid-lent, being the 20th March, 1517, and shipped from Rye, in Sussex, for Dieppe, in Normandy, which he reached in the evening. He very much summarises the early part of his journey, telling us nothing about Paris, except that he walked out to St. Denis one day, and that he left it on the 29th March, "about noon." He reached Lyons on the Monday after Palm Sunday, and immediately applied himself to see the sights, the chief of them being an emerald cup, said to have been used at the Last Supper. Leaving Lyons on Tuesday, he reached Agnebelleto on Thursday morning, the 9th April, and in the afternoon "passed over an ill and a grievous mount called Mount

Gobylyn." He evidently thought nothing of what we call the charms of mountain scenery; for a little further on he again mentions a mountain with horror. At Chambery he heard a doctor preach "a famous sermon," which began at 5 in the morning and continued till 9. He appears to have been surprised at the emotion displayed by the congregation. They fell down on their knees at the sight of a crucifix, and cried with a lamentable voice. "Marvell it was to see." Did he think of the stolid faces of the Suffolk yeomen who "sat under" himself at home?

At St. Jean de Maurienne, "St. John Muryan" in the MS., he shows some signs of scepticism when describing the relics. "There is as they say it the finger of St. John Baptist which he noted or showed Christ when he said, *Ecce Agnus Dei*." But as a rule

his faith, or rather his credulity, was strong. He spent
Easter at St. John's, and on Easter Tuesday made
his journey over Mont Cenis, and reached Suza :
" and there I rest me, for I was weary and my horse
also, for the great labour that I had the same morning
in passing over the evil and grievous 'Mounte
Senes.'" The next day, however, he reached Turin,
"a fair city and university"; and on Friday, the 17th,
he entered Milan, where he remained during the
next three days, visiting the churches and monasteries, and inspecting the relics. "Item," he says,
" in an old church not far from the Castle of Milan,
is a solitary and dilectable place where lies the holy
body of St. Ambrose." On Monday, the 20th, he
left Milan in the afternoon and rode to Pavia, where
he visited the tomb of Lionel of Antwerp, the
second son of Edward III., whose remains were

afterwards removed to England. This concluded the land journey, and on the following day he notes, "I sold my horse, and my saddle, and my bridle."

On Wednesday, the 21st April, he embarked at Pavia, on the Po, and arrived at Placentia, or "Pleasaunce" in the evening. There he laid in provisions and "stuffed himself" with wine, bread, and other provisions. "On Monday, the 27th, he reached Ferrara: "It is a good city, and well and substantially edified," he remarks, and goes on to say that on the following morning "we went on foot five miles to a little village that stands on the water, called Francolina: there I took a bark with merchants of Venice:" and about three o'clock in the afternoon of Wednesday, 29th April, "we came to the goodly and famous city of Venice. There I was well at ease, for there was nothing that I

B

desired to have but I had it shortly. At Venice, at the first house I came to except one, the good man of the house said he knew me by my face that I was an Englishman. And he spoke to me good English. Then I was joyous and glad, for I saw never Englishman from the time I departed out of Paris to the time I came to Venice, which is seven or eight hundred miles."

"The relics at Venice," he continues, "cannot be numbered"; and it would be tedious to follow him round the various churches, chapels, monasteries, and tombs which he visited. In one place he forgot the names of the saints whose remains he had been venerating, and enters in his diary "two other holy bodies whose names be written in the book of life." He never mentions the canals and gondolas, but he saw Venice in her glory, and was present at many great ceremonies, some of which he details at full length. But first he was anxious about his passage to the Holy Land, and appears to have attached himself to a large party of pilgrims similarly bound. On "the 7th of May, the Invention of the Holy Cross, the patron"—probably a kind of sixteenth century Cook, who "personally conducted" travellers to Palestine—"the patron of a new goodly ship, with other merchants, desired us pilgrims that we would come aboard and see his ship within, which ship lay before St. Mark's Church. And about eight o'clock we went all into St. Mark's Church, and after that we went all into the aforesaid ship. There they made us goodly cheer with divers subtleties"—subtleties were, for the most part dishes made up into fantastic forms, into castles and figures of saints—"as comfits and march panes, and sweet wines." The following day they visited another ship which lay five miles from Venice, and the patron "provided for us a marvellous good dinner, where we had all manner of good victuals and wines, and then we returned to Venice again." He tells also of what he saw at the Arsenal, the great number of fine ships, "besides those that be in voyage in the haven." Twenty-three new galleys were being constructed, and "there were working daily upon these galleys a thousand men and more. There be working daily at the same arsenal in a place that is in length 1,080 feet, more than a hundred men and women that do nothing daily but make ropes and cables. There in that castle the merchants showed unto us all manner of artillery and engines that might be devised for war, either by sea or else by land, such as great guns, that some of them be divided in two parts and some in three parts joined together by 'vyres,'"—evidently "wires," or hoops, of thinner metal—"marvel it is to see," he continues, and "many houses and chambers full of guns both great and small, brigatines, cross bows, swords, bills, halberds, spears, moorspikes, with all other things that is required necessary for war." He made an excursion to Padua by water, and dwells rapturously on the relics he saw there, including the finger of St. Luke with which he painted the Blessed Virgin, and three lockers full of bones of the Holy Innocents. Returning to Venice he went "to a place of Nuns which is called St. John Zachary," and there, "in a coffer behind the high altar, lies the holy body of Zachary, the father of St. John the Baptist." In "another church lies the holy body of St. Lucy the Virgin.

Ye may see perfectly her body and her paps." He next assisted at a grand festival held in honour of the Marquis of Mantua—Francesco Gonzaga, who died in 1519—the father of the first Duke, and Torkington goes at full length into a narrative of the masses, processions, and religious services of all kinds which were held. In addition to these there were celebrations of a more secular character, and we may select a few notes from the many pages devoted to feasts, concerts, and theatrical performances.

First of all, he witnessed the Marriage of the Sea. "The Duke"—that is the Doge—"with great triumph and solemnity, with all the Seniory went in their *Archa Triumphali*, which is in manner of a galley of a strange fashion and wondrous stately, etc. And the Marquis of Mantua was with them in the aforesaid galley. And so they rowed into the Sea, with the assistance of their Patriarch, and there espoused the Sea with a ring. The espousal words be, *In signu veri perpetuique dominii.* And therewith the Duke let fall the ring into the Sea, the process and the ceremonies whereof were too long to write." The Doge of Venice at this time was Leonardo Loredano. He had filled his exalted office since 1501, and survived the year of Torkington's Pilgrimage till 1521. His portrait by John Bellini is one of the chief ornaments of our National Gallery. Torkington goes on to describe the Doge and the Marquis at dinner :—" At which dinner there was eight courses of sundry meats, and at every course the trumpets and the minstrels come in before them. There was exceeding much plate, as basins, ewers wondrous great and of a strange fashion; every four persons had a basin and an ewer to wash their hands; also there was a great vessel of silver, and it had at every end round rims gilt, and it was four cornered, and it had at every end four rings that two men might bear it between them for to cast out the water of their basins when they had washed their hands. And while they sat at dinner there was part of the Duke's Chapel singing divers ballads, and sometime they sung with organs; and after that there came one of the trumpeters, and he played with the organs all manner of measure, the (most) excellent, cunning man that ever I heard with divers instruments, I heard or never saw before. And when dinner was done, the Duke sent to the pilgrims great basins full of marchpanes, and also comfits and malmsey, and other sweet wines, as much as any man would eat and drink."

Then followed theatrical performances and danc-
ing. "There came one that was disguised, and he
jested before the Duke, and the Marquis, and the
company, and made them very merry. And after
that there came dancers, and some of them disguised
in women's clothes, that danced a great while. And
after them came tumblers, both men and children,
the most marvellous fellows that ever I saw, so
much that I cannot write it." A long description
follows of a religious procession on Corpus Christi
Day, in which there were "pageants of the old law
and the new law joining together," and other rep-
resentations, and "between every of the pageants
went little children of both kinds," dressed as angels
in cloth of gold and crimson velvet "bearing in
their hands rich cups or other vessels of gold and
silver, richly enamelled and gilt, full of pleasant

flowers and well smelling ; which children cast the flowers on the lords and pilgrims." In short, Venice at the beginning of the 16th century must have been to the rest of the world one of the most interesting and delightful places of resort. Torkington sums up its characteristics in a single sentence :— "The richness, the sumptuous building, the religious houses, and the stablishing of their justices and councils, with all other things that maketh a city glorious, surmounteth in Venice above all places that ever I saw."

He and his companions departed from Venice in a little boat on Sunday the 14th June, " which boat brought us," he says, " to the ship that lay four mile without the castles, a good new ship which never made journey before, of 800 tons ; the name of the Patron was called Thomas Dodo." After

two days they made sail, but with "scarce wind."
On the following Sunday they had only reached
"the Gulf of Sana, that is the entry into Hungary."
Passing on along the coast of "Slovonania" and
Albania, and the wind being favourable, they sailed
by Corfu without touching, but the Patron pointed
out to Torkington "two strong castles standing
upon two rocks"; and he adds, "I trow they had
no where so strong a place, that is in Greece : and
the Turkish main land lieth within two or three
miles of them. And undoubtedly the said Corfu
is the key, entry, and hold for the surety of the said
Venetians' sails and ships and country about ; and
before any other they have in those parts." He
was right in this surmise, as the Turks found soon
after : for they spent their full strength against it
vainly in 1537, and again a few years later, but

Corfu continued in Venetian occupation till the fall of the republic. Torkington goes on to note, "there grows small raisins that we call raisins of Corans: they grow chiefly in Corinth, called now Corona, in Morea, to whom St. Paul wrote many epistles." On the 27th they reached Zante, where they landed. It was also at that time occupied by Venice, and they met with two galleys which had left home a month before them on a Turkish embassy, "and they carried with them riches and pleasures, as cloth of gold, and crimson velvet, and other things more than I know." Our pilgrim complains of Zante, not we must suppose without cause, "there is the greatest wines and strongest that ever I drank in my life." He visited the castle, where the captain made him good cheer, and showed him the walls, "sore bruised and broken" by an earthquake in the previous April. On the last day of June they passed Cerigo, the ancient Cythera—"in the same isle was Venus born "—and on Thursday, 2nd July, the ship arrived at Candia. "It is otherwise called Crete : there be right ill people." Fortunately they encountered some English merchants, who made them good cheer and filled their bottles with muscadel. Of Crete, he remarks, that here " was music first found, and also tourneys and exercise of arms first found on horseback. There was law first put in writing. Armour was first there devised and found, and so was remes (oars) and rowing in boats. In Candia there grow great vines and specially of Malmsey and Muscadel. In the same isle was Saturnus born." He goes on to say that in Candia is the old church whereof Titus was Bishop, " to whom Pole wrott Epystyllis," and that he saw there "the head of the said Titus covered with silver and gold; it is there exceedingly hot." The Venetians are lords of Crete, "and every year or every other year is chosen a Duke by the same Venetians." The Turks, after a war which lasted four and twenty years succeeded in conquering this fine island in 1669, one of the last of their acquisitions in the Mediterranean; but they have long since reduced it to a condition of the utmost misery. It must be observed that the inhabitants professed while they were under Venice to prefer the Turks. Torkington, whose knowledge of the Bible seems to have been quite rudimentary, quotes St. Paul's disparaging notice of the Cretans,* itself a quotation from Epimenides, and says it is to be found in *Actibus Apostolorum.*

---

* Titus i. 12.

On Sunday, the 5th July, the pilgrims sailed for
Rhodes, passing Patmos the next day, and "St.
Nicholas of Carthe" on Tuesday, "whereas be tools
made of iron that never lose their edge by miracle
of St. Nicholas, as they say: I saw it not." As
Patmos and Ceos lie far out of the way between
Crete and Jaffa, our diarist was probably the victim
of his credulity here, but he was evidently getting
a little more cautious, especially about Greek saints,
though the "Patron" apparently succeeded in
deceiving them so far that they did not go near
Rhodes, for fear of the Turks, who in fact took
the place four years later, but do not seem to
have been actually besieging it then, as we shall
see further on in the diary. On Saturday, the 11th
July, the pilgrims first caught sight of the Holy
Land, about 4 o'clock in the afternoon. "Then the

mariners sung the Litany, and after that all the pilgrims with a joyful voice sang *Te Deum Lawidamus* " (*sic*) and thanked heaven for the sight.

The ship anchored at Jaffa, on Sunday, 12th July, and a messenger was sent to Jerusalem, to the Warden of the Mount Sion Convent, to come and conduct the party "as the custom is." While they waited Torkington made some observations as to the place. "At Jaffa beginneth the Holy Land; at this haven Jonas the prophet took the sea." Then follows an account of St. Peter's residence here, and he goes on: "This Jaffa was sometime a great city, as it appeareth by the ruin of the same, but now there standeth never an house, but only two towers, and certain caves under the ground. And it was one of the first cities of the world founded by Japheth, Noe's son, and beareth yet his name." The pilgrims were allowed to land at three o'clock on Wednesday the 15th, when the "father warden of Bethlehem came to us with lords of Jerusalem," and in a short time an arrangement was made with the Turks as to what sum the patron was to pay for the party. As they landed they "were received by the Turks and Saracens, and put into an old cave by name and tale, their scrivenor even writing our names man by man as we entered in the presence of the said lords. And there," he continues, "we lay in the same grot or cave all night upon the stinking stable ground, as well night as day, right evil entreated by the said Turkish Moors." The next afternoon, however, they were permitted to start : "we took three asses, and rode to Rama the same night." Being received into the hospital built by Duke Philip of Burgundy, they found nothing but bare walls and floors, "except only a well of good fresh water, which was much to our comfort. Nevertheless," he adds, "there come to us Jacobins and other feigned Christian people of sundry sorts, that brought to us mats, for our money, to lie on ; and also bread, sodden eggs, and sometimes other victuals, as milk, grapes, and apples." There they rested till six o'clock on Friday afternoon, when the Turkish soldiers dragged them out to a field, where there were two towers, and where they had to lie all night on the bare ground. Early on Saturday morning they started again, and after a mid-day rest "underneath the olive trees" arrived at Jerusalem about six or seven of the clock at afternoon." They were received into the hospital of St. James on Mount Sion, and were entertained with considerable hospitality by the friars, "for the which every man pilgrim recompensed the said friars at their devotion." One of the friars was daily told off to show them "the holy places within the holy land," and the Warden "exhorted every man to confession and repentance, and so to visit the said holy places in cleanness of life."

The next section of Torkington's Diary is taken up with such entries as these: "We went to the house where the sins of Mary Magdalen were forgiven. Thereby is another house that some time was a fair church . . . . And in a vault underneath is the very self place where our Blessed Lady was born. And there is plenary remission. The stones of that place where our Lady was born is remedy and consolation to women that travail of child." Or, "St. Helena builded a church there, but it is down ; and the Saracens have often attempted to build there, but their edifying would not stand in no wise." We must refer the reader curious in the legendary topography of Jerusalem and its environs, to the diary itself. The pilgrims seem to have believed all or nearly all they were told ; and Torkington notes with special satisfaction the places where "clean remission" was promised. For the rest, we may notice one legend and pass on to the return journey. "We descended down by the vale of Solomon's temple ; and first we came to *Torrens Cedron*, which in summer time is dry, and in winter, and specially in Lent, it is marvellous flowing with rage of water that cometh with great violence through the Vale of Josophat. And it runs between the city and the Mount of Olivet, and it is called as it is before,

Torrens Cedron. And over the said water St. Helena made a bridge of stone, which is yet thereover. And many years before the passion of Christ, there lay over the said water a tree for a foot bridge, whereof the holy cross was afterwards made. This seeing, the Queen of Sheba, by the spirit of prophecy, when she passed that way she would not tread thereupon, but waded through the water, seeing that the Saviour of all the world should suffer His death upon that tree. There is clean remission." Of Jerusalem he observes, briefly, that it is "a fair eminent place, for it standeth upon such a ground that from whence soever a man cometh there he must needs ascend"; and again, "I saw never city nor other place have so fair prospects." From Jerusalem he visited Bethlehem and the hill country of Judea, which he calls "the mounts of

Jude," where he saw a fountain "where our Blessed Lady was wont many times to wash her clothes and the clothes of our Blessed Saviour in His childhood."

On Monday (27th July) "that was *Septem Dormientium*" they bade farewell to Mount Sion, and "took humble leave of the holy places," and after waiting long for their asses, "with right light and joyous hearts, by warning of our dragman * and guides, the same day at nine of the clock in the morning we found all ready, the lords, Turks, and Saracens, Mamelukes, as well of Jerusalem as of Rama, and others with their folks to a great number, to conduct us to Jaffa." They rested in the hospital at Rama as before, "being right weary of

---

* This early use of the word is interesting. The root is connected with the Hebrew "targum," and targoman, dargoman, or dragoman all over the east means an interpreter.

that journey, for the beasts that we rode upon (were) right weak, and right simple, and evil trimmed to journey." The following day they went on, but were detained four hours by the cruelty of the Turks, "and there we lay in the sand, and the sun burning exceedingly hot, which was greatly to our pain. And there we were right evil entreated by the Turks and Saracens, many ways, and in great fear, which were too long to write. The same night with great difficulty and much patience we were delivered aboard into our ship. And there we lay at anchor Wednesday and Thursday all day. The cause was there came many infidels and brought many sundry things into our ship. And Friday, the last day of July, about five of the o'clock in the morning, we made sail towards Cyprus with right great joy and solace."

Though the ship reached Cyprus in four days an unaccountable delay took place there, and for a month no progress was made. On the 25th of August one of the pilgrims died, namely Robert Crosse, of London, pewterer, and was buried in Salamis or Constantia, which Torkington calls Salyns, near Famagosta. "And xxvii. day of August, deceased Sir Thomas Toppe, a priest of the west country, and was cast over the board, as was many more, whose souls God assoil. And then there remained in the ship four English priests more." They reached Rhodes on the 25th September, and when they sailed from thence our diarist appears to have been left behind ill. "There myself lay sick by the space of six weeks;" but the Knights were good and hospitable, and he specially mentions " Sir Thomas Newporte, Master William

Weston* and Sir John Bowthe." He remained at
Rhodes till 12th November, when he sailed in a
Rhodian vessel ; but contrary winds detained it a
month, and on the 3rd January a heavy gale put it in
great "joyparty." The passengers were bound for
Messina, in Sicily, and during the storm made vows
of pilgrimages to various shrines, "some to our lady
of Walsingham, some to St. Thomas of Canterbury,
we that were Englishmen." They were driven up
and down in the Gulf of Venice, as he calls the
Adriatic, for a week or more, "and sore we were

---

* This was probably the same Weston who became the last
Lord Prior of Clerkenwell, and died of grief at the suppression :
"So it fortuned that upon the 15th May, 1540, being Ascension
day, and the same day of the dissolution of the house, he was
dissolved by death, which struck him to the heart at the first
time, when he heard of the dissolution of his order."—*Newcourt's
Repertorium*, i. 658.

afraid to be driven into Barbaria, where dwelleth
our mortal enemies as Turks, Mamelukes, Saracens,
and other infidels." At length they sighted land,
and got to Cephalonia, " under the Venetians, and
when we should have taken the port suddenly fell
down and died the pilot of our ship." There they
lay twenty-five days, and sailed again on the 30th
January, but the wind rising drove them to Corfu,
which they were obliged to pass, but anchored on
the Albanian coast, on an island which Torkington
calls Swafana, where " we abode five days ; and
divers Knights of the Rhodes went on land with
their hand guns, and slew horse for their hawks
that were in the ship; there were in the ship a
hundred hawks and more." On the 12th February,
they landed at Corfu, a place with which our pilgrim was delighted : " the fairest ground that ever

I saw in my life." There he witnessed a Jewish wedding, which he describes, and on Friday, 26th February, the ship sailed for "Myssena, Cecyll."

The wind was still strong, and it was not until 8th March that they reached the Calabrian coast, where Torkington was much surprised at the fine cliffs. " Also over the water on the other side, which is distant from Calabria 23 miles, is the Isle of Sicily, in the which isle by the sea side is *Mons Ethneus* (Mount Etna), which burneth both day and night— ye may see the smoke come out of the top of it. There came out of this hill fire running down like as it had been a flood of water into the city which standeth by the sea side, and burnt many houses and also ships that were in the haven, and put the city which is called Catania in great jeopardy, where the holy body of St. Agatha lies. And by the miracle of the veil of St. Agatha the city afore rehearsed was preserved." The travellers landed in Calabria on the 11th March, hired horses and mules and rode to Reggio, where they rested, and crossed the following day to Messina, where they remained a week and then proceeded by a coasting boat, a hundred miles towards Naples. On Sunday, 21st, they landed and hired horses. Passing through Salerno, "a fayer citee stondyng on the see syde," they reached Naples, on Saturday. Torkington says nothing about the scenery, but was much struck with the castle—"the gates be goodly, and made of white marble"—and with the Grotto of Pausilippo. "Without the city is an horse way under neath a mountain by the space of a mile, a marvellous cave in the ground, which we rode through the same Palm Sunday after mass, towards

Rome." He reached Rome on the 31st March, and bought a horse which carried him the rest of his land journey; but he tells us nothing else about the Holy Week during which he remained there, because both Rome itself and the way from it "is known perfectly I know with many sundry persons in England, and therefore I do not write it." On Sunday after the Ascension "we shipped our horses at Calais. On Monday that was the 17th April, we came to Dover, and lay there all night. Tuesday before Whit Sunday we came to Canterbury, to St. Thomas's mass, and there I offered and made an end of my pilgrimage. *Deo Gracias.*" He adds some notes on the time occupied. "We were out of England in our said pilgrimage the space of an whole year, five weeks, and three days." The book concludes with a description of the Temple of

Solomon, and Torkington seems to have had no
doubt that the Dome of the Rock was the identical
building erected by Herod.

Thys ys the begynnyng of the Pylgrymage of Syr Rychard Torkyngton Perſon of Mulberton in Norffolke. And how he went towardys Iheruſalem all a lone to the tyme he came to Veneſſe.

Torkington's Pilgrimage.

ffyrst the ffryday a for mydlent, that was Seynt Cuthberdy's
Day, And the xx Day of Marche in the vii yer of Kyng
Herri the viiith And the yer of ower Lorde God
mˡcccccxvij,* a bowte viij of the cloke the same mornyng,
I shipped at Rye, in Sussex, And the same Day a browte
x of the cloke at nyghte I londed at Depe, in Normandy, And
ther I lay in the Shippe all nyght. Satirday that was Seynt
Benett's Day I cam on londe in to Depe, And ther I taryed all
Day.

Midlente sonnday, the xxij Day of Marche, a browte xj of the
cloke, I toke my hors at Depe and rode to Totys † wher I baytyd
And so to Rone ‡ the same nyght, where I bode munday all Day

Twesday, the xxiiij Day of March, I departyd from Rone to
Cuys to Diner, And to Myny the nyght.

---

* Usually reckoned 1516.   † Tôtes.   ‡ Rouen.

Wedynsday, the Anunciacion of ower lady, to Povntese* to Dine and to Parys the same nyght, wher I bode Thursday, ffryday, and Satyrday.

The thursday I went to Seynt Denys on ffote, wher I offerd and sawe the relyqwys, and so retornyd a gayne the same nyght to Parys.

Passion Sonday, the **xxix** Day of Marche, abowte none, I departyd from Parys. And the vj Day of Aprill I cam to Tarrare,† wher I passyd an ill mountayne all a lone. And to Labrylle. ‡

The munday aftyr Palme sonday I cam to Lyon, which was a long Jorney, xij scor myle and **x**.

At lyons I visityd the Reliques at the yle wher Sent Anne lyes and longious. ‖ Ther ys also a Cuppe of an Emerawde stone, wherof ower Savyor Crist Drank at hys Mawdy.

At the Grey ffreres the lyes the Holy body of Seynt Bonaventur in Lyon.

Tewysday, the vij Day of Aprill, at ij of the cloke at aftyr none, I Departyd ffrom Lion.

Thursday that was the ix Day of Aprill, I com to Agnebelleto. § The aftyr none I passed ovyer an ill and a grevows Mounte callyd mounte Gobylyn, the same nyght I com to Cambery ¶ with inne the mountis. Wher I bode ffryday and hard Divine service.

---

* Pontoise.   † Tarare.   ‡ La Verpilliere?
‖ Perhaps Longinus.   § Probably Aiguebelle.   ¶ Chambery.

Ther in a Castyll ys a ffayer Churche where ys the sudary of ower Savyor Crist Jhu.

And ther I hard a ffamus Sermon of a Doctor which began a v of the cloke in the mornyng and contynuyd tyll it was ix of the clok.

In hys sermon at on tyme he had a balys* in hys hond, a nother tyme a schorge, the iij^de tyme a Crowne of thorne, the iiij^th tyme he shewyd the pepyll a pictur poyntyd on a clothe, of the passion of our lorde. And after that he shewyd them the ymage of god crucyfyed vpon a crosse, and thanne all the peple bothe yong and old they fell downe vpon ther knes and cryed with lamentable voce, oman,† the precher, the peple they weppe, marvell it was to see.

Estern evyn, I com to Seynt John Muryan,‡ ther I a bode Ester Day all Day and hard Devine service; in that Cite ys a Cathedrall Church of seculer Prests. Ther I sey many Reliquis. Ther ys as they say yt the ffynger of Seynt John Baptiste whych he notyd or shewyd crist Jhu whanne he seyd Ecce Agnus Dei, ther I offerd.

Ester munday, the xiij Day of Aprill, to Seynt Michell and so to Seynt Andrew to Dyner. The aftyr none to lynnygbur to bede.

Estern tewysday to Suza to Diner, And the I rest me, for I was were and my hors also ffor the grett labor that I had the

---

* Probably a chalice.   † Amen.   ‡ St. Jean de Maurienne.

same mornyng in passing over the evyll and grevows mounte Senes,* yet I come the same nyght to sent Ambros to my logeyng.

Ester Wedynesday, the xv Day of Aprill, to Turyn, a fayer Cite and Universite, and to Shewans† the same nyght.

Thursday, the xvj Day of Aprill, to Salys‡ to Diner, And to Wersell ‖ the same night.

ffriday, the xvij Day of Aprill, to Novera,§ and the same nyght to the grett Cite of Myllane.

Ther I a bode Satyrday, Sunday and munday, All Day. The in a Chirche of Seynt Silvester ys many grett reliquis, a pece of the vesture of our blyssyd lady. And also of Seynt Jamis, a nother relik of ij of the Innocentis, Also on of the thornys that ower lord was crownyed with. The erth of the Sepultur of ower lady, the staff of Seynt Ambros, the Gyrdell of Seynt Ambros, also the hede of Seynt Barbere, And many moo Reliquis it ys to long too wrytte.

Also ther ys a grett Churche of our Blyssyd lady, And ovyr the hye Auter in the Roff or toppe of the Churche ys a syne of a sterr of golde, and in the mydys of the Sterr ys on of naylis that ower Savyr Crist was crucifyed with. Ther brenne lampes a bowth it that ye may se in perfyghtly.

Item, in an old Chyrch nott fer ffrom the Castell of Myllane,

---

* Mont Cenis.   † Perhaps Chivaso.   ‡ Saluggia.
‖ Vercelli.   § Novara.

ys a Solatory and a Dilectable Place, wher lyes the Holy Body of Seynt Ambros, And ther I offerd, And it ys callyd Sanctus Ambrosius.

Munday, the xx day of Aprill, the aftyr none, I rode to Papia or Pavia, a cite and universite, ther lyes Seynt Austyn, the grett Doctor, in a howse of Religion, of Chanons reguler, and ffryers Austyns, all being withine the circuite and precincte of Place, they have nevthelesse severall Cloysters and severall logyngs. ·But they kepe All ·her Divine service in on qwere all to gedyr.

In the same church lyeth Lyonell, the second sonne of king Edward the iij^de, honorable, vpon whose tumbe ys wretyn, Sanguine insignis fuerat vell floribus armis. Ossa Leoneti continet iste lapis.

In thys cite I abode tewysday, all Day and all nyght.

In the same Cite I sold my horse, and my sadyll, and brydell.

Wedynsday, the xxj Day of Aprill, I toke a barke att the forseyd Pavia, vpon the Ryver which ys callyd Poo ; the same nyght I cam to Placiencia or Plesaunce ; ther I stuffed me w^t wyne and bred and other caseles* as me thowght necessary for me at that tyme.

Seynt Gorgys Day to Cremena, a ffayer Cite, and ther I a bode all nyght.

Seynt Markes Day to Dosor.†

---

* I have failed to find a meaning for "caseles."   † Caorso?

Sunday, the xxvj Day of Aprill, I passyd by Mantua, And so to the towne which ys callyd Ryver.* And ther I lay all nyght.

Munday, the xxvij Day of Aprill, to fferare,† and ther I lay all nyght, it ys a good Cite, And well and substancially Edifyed.

Tewysday, Erly in the mornyng, we went on fote v myle to a lytyll velage that stande on the watir called ffranccolyno, ther I toke a barke with Marchauns of Venyse, the same nyght we lay att Corbala.

Lityll above fferare the Poo departeth in to two parts, The oon goth to fferare, And so in too the see, And the other parte to Padow.

Wedynsday, the xxix Day of Aprill, ij howrys afore Day, we toke the same barke ageyne, And a none we left all the Poo, and toke ower course by a lytyll Ryver that cometh to the same, called the ffosse, made and cutte owte by hande, whych browght vs overwhart in to a nother Ryver called Latyze, ‡ that cometh from Verone And Trent, And yett w^t inne a whyle we traversed owt of that Ryver into a nother lytell Ryver, whiche browght vs overwhart a gen in to Latyze, which Latize browght vs in to chose vpon the see callyd in latyn Claudin, xxv myle ffrom Venys, and ther Dyned.

The same Day we sayled toward Venys, and a bowt iij of the cloke at aftyr none we com to the goodly and ffamose cite of Venys.

---

* The Riviera, or quay of Mantua. † Ferrara. ‡ Adige.

Ther I was well at ese, ffor ther was no thyng that I Desyred to have but I had it shortly.

At Venyse, at the fyrst howse that I cam to except ooń, the good man of the howse seyd he knew me by my face that I was an englysshman. And he spake to me good englyssh, thane I was Jous and glade, ffor I saw never englyssh man ffrom the tyme I Departed owt of Parys to the tyme I cam to Venys, which is vij or viij C myles.

The Reliquies at Venys canne not be nowmbred. Ther lyeth Seynt Elyn, Seynt Barbara, Seynt Luke, Seynt Roke, Seynt Zachary, Seynt Jervas and Prothase. And many other Seyntis and grett reliques.

May Day we went to Seynt Elyn and offerd ther, She lith in a ffayer place of religion of whith monks ye may se hyr face perfythly hyr body ys Covered with a cloth of whith Sylke.

The iiide Day of May, the Invencion of the holy Crosse. The patrone of a new goodly sheppe with other Marchauntes Desyred vs Pylgrymys that we wold com a bord and see hys shippe with inne, which Shippe ley afor Seynt Markys chirche, And a bowyte viij of the Cloke we went all in to Seynt Markes Churche, And aftyr that we went all in to the fforseyd Shippe. Ther they mad vs goodly Chere wt Diverse Sotylties as Comfytes and Marche Panys, And Swete Wynes.

Also the vth Day of May, the Patrone of a nother Shippe whiche lay in the see v myle from Venys, he Desyered vs all Pylgrymys that we wold come and se hys Shippe And the same

Day we went all with hym, And ther he provydyd for vs a mervelous good Dyner, wher we had all maner of good viteales, And wynes, And thanne we retornyed to Venys a geyne.

At the Archinale ther we saw in makyng $\frac{xx}{iii}$ * new galyes and galye Bastards, And galye Sotyltes, besyd they that be in viage in the haven.

Ther ys Werkying Dayly upon thez Galyes a ml men† and moo.

Ther be werkying Daly at the same Archinale, in a place that ys in lengthe ml lxxx ffote, mo thanne an C men and women that Doo no thyng Dayly but make Ropes and Cables.

Ther in that Castyll the Marchauntes schewyd vn to vs all maner of artyllary And Ingynes that myght ben Devysed ffor warre, other be see or ellys be londe.

As grett gunnes that sum of them be Divided in ij partes and sum in iij partes Joynyd to gedyr be vyres, marvell it ys to see.

Also ther ys many howses and Chaumbers full of gunnes, bothe grett and small, bryganynes, Crosbowys, Swardys, byllys, halbardes, Sperys, Moryspekys, with all other thynges that ys required necessary for warre.

Wedynsday, the vj Day of May, we went by watir to Padua, by the Ryver of Brente, And there we visite and Sawe many Reliquies, As Seynt Antoni, whiche was a grey ffryer, And lith

---

* Three score.   † 1000 men.

Rygth ffayer in the body of the Churche, In the Vestrye thɛr ys an herse that stonde full of Chalys to the nowmbyr of $\frac{xx}{iiii}$* or $\frac{xx}{v}$,† wher in ys closyd many grett Reliquies, A rybbe of the syd of Seynt Bonaventur, which translate the holy body of Seynt Antony, And also the tong of Seynt Antony, yet ffayer and ffressh whiche tong he convertyd mych peple to the ffeythe of Crist.

Also in the Abbey of Seynt Justine virgyne, a place of blake monkys, ryght Delectable And also Solytary, Ther lithe the holy body of Seynt Justine, And Seynt Luke, and Seynt Mathew, And ther we see the ffynger of Seynt Luke that he wrotte the holy gospell with. And also the table of ower blyssyd lady, which Seynt Luke poyntyd with hys owen hande, berying her sone in hyr Armys, it ys seyd who so ever be hold thys pictur of our blyssyd lady, Devowtly onys in hys lyff he shall never be Deprivyd ffrom the syght of hyr evlastyng.

Also ther ys ij locures ‡ of iij quarterys of a yard long ffull of bonys of Innocentis whyche kyng Herrodys slew ffor malyce that he bar to Criste.

Thursday, the vij Day of May, we retornyed by the same watir of Brent to Venese ageyne.

Item at Venese ys a place of Nonnys which ys callyd Seynt Johnis Zachari, in a Coffer by hynd the hith Auter lies the holy body of Zachari, ffather of Seynt John Baptiste, And other ij holy bodys whose namys be wretyng in libro vite.

---

* Four score.   † Five score.   ‡ Lockers.

In the Abbey of Seynt George ther we sey many Reliquies of holy Seyntes, bothe Martyres and Virgines, the holy Bodyes and Armys of them, the ffaces, ther ffyngers, the tethe of them, it ys grett mervell to see, Ther is a parte of the hede of Seynt George, hys left Arme with the holl hande. The Arme of Seynt Lucie, The Bodys of Seynt Cosme and Damiane.

May Day we went to Seynt Elyne, to a place of Whith Monkes that stande in the See. Ther she lyeth in a fayer Chapell Closyd in a Coffer, hyr face bare and nakyed that ye may se it perfyghtly, which Seynt Elyne ffond the Crosse at Jherusalen, Also ther lyes upon hyr brest a lytyll crosse made of the holy crosse, Also the Tunbe of Constantini magni, Sone of Seynt Elyn, And a bone of Seynt Mary Mawdleyn.

In the Monastery of blake monkys callyd Seynt Nicholas De Elio, Ther lyes the body of Seynt Nicholas as they sey, Also oon of the Pottis that ower lord turnyd watir in to wyne, The staff of Seynt Nicholas that he vsed whanne he was Bushoppe.

In the Monastery callyd Accusechirii* lyes the body of Seynt Barbare, Also in a nother Auter ys a bone of Seynt Cristofer. Also in the Church callyd Sancta Marina lies the holy body of hyr De qua miracula vitaspatrum leguntur.

Also in a nother Church lies the holy body of Seynt Luce Virgyn, ye may see perfyghtly hyr body and hyr Papys.

---

* Perhaps "Chiesa Zaccaria," the "Seynt Johnis Zachari" named above.

In the Curche of Seynt Marke ther ys many grett Reliquies and Jowellys, ther ys a gret Chalis of fine gold of Curius werke, est with many precius stonys which ys in heyght iij quarters of a yard it ys to large to vse at messe. But they vse it in ornyng * the Auter at principall tymes.

Ther be also iij grett Sensurys Of gold as hye as the Chalys ys, and peyer of grett Candylstykes, a mong other a wonderfull gretnesse that be rygtht Curiusely wrogth and arn † fyne gold garnyshed over all with stones of gret Pryse.

Ther be also xij Crownes of fine gold, And a Riche Cappe which every Duk ys Crowned with at hys ffrist Intrononyzacions. The price of all with Crownes Pectorales. And a Coppe ys inestymable, ffor they be full sett with precious stunys of grett valor that may be.

Also ther be viij grett Copys of fyne gold garnyshed over with precius stonys.

All these thyngs I sawe whanne they war shewyd to the Marchose of Mantua,† which browght with hym many Knyghtes and Gentylmen in Riche aperell.

Thys Don we passed owt of the Vestre, and so to the hye Auter, And a non it was sett opyn, And ther war ij torchis brynyng. The Marchose had a Candyll govyn to him in hys hande bornyng. The gold, the precius stonys in the Auter when they Glysteryd And shone, it was grett mervell to See.

---

* Adorning.   † An urn.
‡ Francis Gonzaga, father of the first Duke of Mantua.

The Richesse, the sumptuous buyldyng, The religius howses and the stabelyssyng of ther Justyces and Counceylles, with all other thynges that makyth a Cite glorius Surmownteth in Venys a bove all places that ever I Sawe.

And specially at ij festis wher at we war present, the on was vpon the Assencion Day. The Duke* with grett Triumphe and solemnyte with all the Senyorye went in ther Archa triumphali, which ys in maner of a sayle of a straange facion and wonder stately, etc.

And the Marchose of Mantua was w^t them in the forseyd Galye.

And so they rowed in to the see, with the assistens of ther Patriarche, And ther Spoused the see with a ryng. The spousall words be In signum veri perpetuique Domini.† And therwith the Duke lete fall the ryng in to the see, the processe and the cery-monyes wherof war to long to wryte.

Thanne thaye Rode to the Abbey of Seynt Nicholas of blake Monkys that stond by juste be them, And all thaye brake ther fastes, And so retornyd a geyne to Venys, To the Dukys palace, Wher they had provyd for them a mervelows Dyner, wher at we Pilgrymes war present and see them servyd. At which Dyner her was viij Corse of soundery metys, And att every Corse the Trunpettes and the mynystrellys com inne a for them.

Ther was excedyng myche plate, As basons, Ewers, wonders

---

* The Doge in 1517 was Leonardo Loredano, who died in 1521.
† *Sic* in MS. Should it not be "Dominii"?

grett And of a straunge facion, every iiij persons had a bason and Ewer to washen ther handes, Also ther was a grett Vesell of Sylver, And it had at every ende rounde rymys gylte and it was iiij cornarde, And it had at every ende iiij ryngs that ij men myght bere it betwyne them ffor to Cast owt the watyr of ther basons whanne they had wasshed ther handys, Ther Dysshys ther platers ther Sawcers, all was of Syliver and gylte.

And while they satt at Dyner ther was parte of the Dukys Chapell singing Dyverse balyttys, And sumtyme they song with Orgones, And aftyr that ther cam on of the Trompetores and he pleyd with the Organs all maner of messur the excellent conyng man that ever I hard with Diverse Instrumets I hard nor never see a ffor.

And whanne Dyner was Don, the Duke sent to the Pilgryms gret basons full of Marchepanys,* And also commfytes and maluysey, And other Swete Wynys as myche as ony man wold ete and Drynke.

This Don ther cam on that was Disgysyd and he gestyd a for the Duke and the Marchose and the company and made them Very mery.

And aftyr that ther cam Dauncers and some of them Disgysyd in women clothes that Daunsyd a gret while.

And after them come Tombelers, both men And children, the marvelows ffelaws that ever I saw So myche that I conne nott writt it.

---

* Biscuits.

The other ffest was oon Corpis xpi Day, wher was the most Solemne pcession that ever I saw. Ther went Pagents of the old law and the new law Joynyng to gedyr. The ffygmyes* of the blyssyd sacrament in such nowmber and so apte and convenient for that ffest that it wold made any man Joyus to se it. And over that it was a grett merveyle to se the grett nowmbre of Religius ffolkes and of Scolys that we call Bachelors or ffelachippys Clothid all in white gramens with Diverse bags† on ther brestis which bar all lights of wondyr goodly facion, And be twyne every of the Pagents went lityll childern of both kynds, gloriusly and rechely Dressed beryng in ther handys ryche Cuppes or other vessales of gold and silver Rychely inamelyd and gylt ffull of plesaunt fflowers and well Smellying which chyldern kest the flowers vpon the lords and pylgrymes. They war Dressed as Aungellis with clothe of gold and crymsyn velvet to order the seyd procession. The forme and manner therof excedyd all other that ever I Saw, so much that I canne nott wryte it.

The Duke Satt in Seynt Markes Churche in ryght hys astate in the Qwer on the ryght syd with senyoryte which they call lords in Riche aparell as purpyll velvet, cremsyn velvet, ffyne Scarlett.

Also all the pylgrymes war commandyd to com in to the ffor seyd Qwer and ther we Satt all on the left syd on the quere. The Duke thus Syttyng with hys lords, the seyd procession be ganne to com be hym a bowte viij of the clok and it was xij or

---

* The sacred elements, from the Latin *figmenta*.   † Badges

the seyd pression myght Com oonys a bowt pessyng by as faste
as they myght goo but on tyme.

Thanne the Duke rose vp with hys lords and company to folow
the fforsayd procession. He commaundyd hys lordys that they
shuld in the procession every oon of them take a Pylgryme on his
Right-hande hys servaunts gevyng to vs grett Candyls of wax,
whych Candelys every Pylgrim bar a-way the procession Doon at
hys owen plesur. We procedyd owt of Seynt Markes Churche,
in to the Dukys pales, and so went procession with inne the seyd
place because it was Reyne wedyr, * And so retornyed in the
Churche a geyne of Seynt Marke and ther made ende of the
seyde Procession.

Sonday aftyr Corpus xpi Day, the xiiij of Jume, we Departyd
from Venys in a lytyll bott whyche bott browght vs to the Shippe
that lay iiij myle withowt the Castellys, a good new shippe whiche
mad never Jorney a fore of viij C tunne, The name of the Patrone
was callyd Thomas Dodo.

Tweaday, the xvj Day of June, whiche was the translacion of
Seynt Richard, a browt v of the Clok in the mornyng we mad
sayle with scace Wynde.

Thursday, the xviij of June, we cam to Ruyne † in Histria, x
myle from Parens,‡ C myle and x from Venys. Ther we went a
lond and lay ther all nyght, ffryday in the mornyng we hard
messe.

---

* Rainy weather.   † Rovigno.   ‡ Parenzo.

Friday, the xix Day of June, a lityll a for nyght, we com all to the Shippe a geyn.

Ther we lay Satyrday all Daye at a naker in the havyn, ventus erat contrarius.

Sonnday a for Midsom day, abowyt vij of the cloke in the mornyng we made Sayle, And passyd by the Costes of Slavone and Histria, And also Pole * which ys xxx myle from Parence, a good havyn ffor many Shippys and galyes towche ther rather thanne at Parence. We Passyd also by Gulfe of Sana, † that yᵌ the entre in to Hungeri.

Munday, that was Seynt Albon's Day, we passyd by the havyn of Jarre. ‡

Midsomerday we passyd by the most strong and myzghty towne callyd Aragouse, ‖ in the Countre of Salvanye or Dalmacie, they hold of no man but of them self. They pay tribute to the Turke whiche marche with inne half a myle of the same towne, it ys the Strongest towne of walls, towers, Bulwerks, waches, and wardes that ever I saw in all my lyff. This Cite ys v C myle ffrom Venys.

Abowte xxx myle by yond Arragouese endith Slovonania, And begyneth Albane, at the town of Budua.

Thursday aftyr MidsomDay, a bowte iiij of the Cloke at aftyr noon we passid by Corfona.§ The wynd made so well for vs

---

* Pola. † Zara ?
‡ More probably this is Zara. ‖ Ragusa. § Corfu.

That we approched nott noon nye non of ther havyns a for-seyd.

At Corfona as the Patrone Shewyd me the be ij strong Castellys, stonding vp on ij Rokkys. They hold of the Venysyans. I trowe they had no wher so strong a place yt ys in Grece. And the Turkes mayne londe lithe with in ij or iij myle of them

And on Dowtyd the seyd Corfona ys the key entre and hold for the suerte of the seyd Venycians Sayles and Shippis and countre a bowte, And be fore any other that they have in those parts. And at the seyd Corfona they speke all Greke and be Grekes in Dede.

Ther growes smale Raysons that we call reysons of Corans, they growe Chefly in Corinth callyd now Corona in Morrea, to whom Seynt Poule wrote many epistelis. Corfo ys the fiyrst yle of Grece, and it ys from Arrogous iij C myle.

At my commying nomward I shall writte mor of the forseyd townnes.

ffryday that was Johns et Pauli we sayled with Ese, wynde styll, in alto Pelago, levyng Grece on the left hand and Barbary on the ryght honde.

These be the parte of the Countres that we passyd by. S. *
Histria, Croacia, Slovonia, Dalmacia, Hilliricum, Corfieu Insula, Dardania Insula, per Achaya, et Albanian per mare, Molon, whiche Countres be all to Grece be yongh Corffew, Aswell the

---

* Scilicet, to wit.

E

mayne londs as the yles, And so Doth bothe Candy and Cypres with many moo, And thanne comyth inn Pathmos Insula, Troya, Constantynapolis, Tracia.

Satyrday, the xxvij Day of Junij, a bowght iiij of the cloke at aftyr noone, we cam to Ganta,* in Grece, and ther we went on londe, And ther we taryed Sonnday, whych ys vnder the Dominacon of the Venycians. Also we mette with ij Galyes of Venys, whiche went owte of Venys a moneth a for vs, whiche Galyes went to the Turke Ambasset, And they Caryed with them Riches and pleasurs, As clothe of gold and Crymsyn velvett, And other thyngs mor than I knewe.

Ther is the grettest wynys and strongest that ever I drank in my lyff.

Sunday, whanne I had dyned I went to the Castyll, which stondyth in the toppe of a Mownte, ther the Captyne of the Castyll made me good Cher, And shewyd to me all the Castyll with in The towers, the wallys are sore brosyd and brokyn with the erthe qwake which was in Aprill last past, And all the yle ys sor trobled with the seyd erthe qwake Dyvse tymes. And it ys Also plenteouse of all maner of thyngs that any man nede to have.

Tewysday, the last Day of June, that was the Commeracion of Seynt Poule, we passed by Modona,† it was but late the Venycians, but now the Turke have it. Ther groweth moche Rumney,

---

* Zante.   † Modon.

And mawnsey. Thys Modona ys CCC myle ffrom Corfona, And from Modona to Candia ys other CCC myle.

Also we passyd by the yle Callyd Cyrygo, it ys directly a yenst the Poynt of Campo Maleo* in Morrea, And in the same yle was Venus borne, And in the some yle ys Delphos, And it ys all in Europa, And so ys all the remnant of Grece, And be yonthe Grece ov a brache of the see ys Asia, where in all most at thentre stonding Troya, whiche ys the Cheffe Porte of the yle of Tenedos that stondeth in the see. And all the Countre of Troya ys the Turkes owen contre by herytaunce. And that countre ys propyrly callyd now Turkey, And non other Neverthelasse he hath lately vsurped Grece with many other Countres, And call them all Turkey.

Over a gens the forseyd yle of Cirigo to the se wardes ys the Stopull of Craggs called in Greke Obaga, for it ys leke an egge.

Thursday, the ij^de Day of Julii, a bowt xj or xij of the Cloke a for non, we com to Candi, itt is callyd otherwyse Crete, ther be ryht Ill Peple, it is vnder the Venyschyans. Ther we ffonde vj or vij englissh Marchaunts whiche made vs good cher. And they gaff to vs at our Deptyng to the Shippe, Muskedele as myche as fyllyd our botellys.

In Candia sive Creta was Musyke fyrst founde. And also Tourneys and exercyse of Armys fyrst founde on horsebake. Ther was lawe fyrst put in wrytyng. Armour was fyrst ther

---

* Cape Malea.

Divisyd and founde, And so was remys and rownyg in bootes. In Candia ther growe grett Vynes, And specially of malwesy and muskadell. In the same yle was Saturnus borne. Primus Creteys Saturnus venit ab oris, etc.

In Candi Also ys the old Churche wherof Titus was Bysshoppe, to whom Pole wrott Epystyllis, I saw the hede of the seyd Titus Coverd w^t sylver and golde, it ys ther excedyngly hoote.

Thes be the Principall Cetees Off Candi, S. Canea, Candida, Aretymo, Sotiglia. And the seyd Ill ys v C myle a bowte, And thys Citee of Candi was sum tyme the habitacule and lordshippe of the Kyng Mynos. At Candi ys a strong Castell and a large and a fayer towne w^t owt the Castell, well wallys strongly, thys Ile ys a grett Ile and a Plenteows of all maner of thyngs. They be Grekes in that Ile, And the Vencions ben Lord ther, And every yer or every other yer ys Chosyn a Duke by the same Venycions.

Ther groweth the Voyne that ys callyd Malweysy and muskedell. Sumtyme ther Dwellyd Cretes yt ys wretyng of them in Actibus aptor,* Cretenses semper mendaces bestie.

In that londe, xxx myle from Candy, ys an old brokyn Citee whiche was callyd Cretina, And a lityll ther be syd stondyth an old Churche which was byldyd in the honor of Jhu Criste And holowyd in the worshipe of Titus Epiis,† to whome Seynt Poule wrott in Actibus Aptor Ad Titum. In thys Ile as they sey ther

---

* Apostolorum. But the text, a quotation from Epimenides, is in Titus i. 12. † Episcopus.

war sumtyme a C Citees and C Kynges, In thys Citee we taryed ij Dayes and an half. And there was grett hete, ffor from May to Halowmesse ther groweth no gresse, It is so brent with the hete of the sone, And thanne abowzt halowmesse begynneth gresse, herbes and flowers to springe, And it ys ther thanne as somor ys in Inglonde. So in wynter it ys temperat, no cold but lityll, ther ys never Snow nor frost with yse, And yf ther cometh any frost with a lityll yse they wyll shew it eche to other ffor a mervell. And fro May tyll the latter ende of October Ther ys no Rayne nor clowdes but ryghte selde.* But ever the sone shyneth ryght cler and hote. And a bowte Seynt Martyns tyme the sonne ys as hote ther as it ys in August in Englond. And so it ys in Rodes and Cipres. And all that Countre Estwarde.

Sonday, the v Day of Julii, a bowghte vj of the Cloke in the mornyng, we made seyle ffrom Candy towardes the Rodes.

Munday, at nyght, we passed by the Ile of Pathmos wher Seynt John wrote the Apocalips, whych Ile we left on ower left hande towardes Grece.

The next Day, tewysday, we passed by the Ile of Seynt Nicholas of Cartha wher as be tooles made of Iron that never lese ther egge by myracle of Seynt Nicholas, As they say, I saw it not.

The same tewysday, we Saylyd ryght Estwardes toward Cipres, And left the Rodes on the left hande, nott aproched ny the rodes by C myle ffor fer of the Turke.

---

* Right seldom.   * Lose their edge.

Ower patrone of the shippe had sent to hym letters at Candy that he shuld toche at the rodes in no wysse. Yf he Dede the Turke wold sone have knowlage. And so to take greet Displesur with vs all, and peraventur putt vs in Joypte* off ower lyffe, ffor of trewthe he ys not content with no man that ys famyliar with the company that ys at the Rodes, ffor that hell broude takys them as hys mortall enimes.

It is from Candy to the rodes iij D myle. And from the Cipres iiij C myle. Sunday, in the mornyng, the v Day of Julii, a bowght v of the Cloke in the Mornyng, we made sayle.

Wedynsday, the viij Day of Julii, we came Cipres, And ther we lay thursday all Day.

ffriday, the x Day of July, a bowght x or xj of the Cloke, we made Sayle.

Satirday, the xj Day of Julii, a bowght iiij of the Cloke at aftyr noon, we had sight of the holy londe. Thanne the Maryners song the letany, And aftyr that all the Pylgryms with a Joyffull voyce song Te Deum Lawid-amus, And thankyd all myghty god that he had goven vs such grace to have onys the sight of the most holy lande.

ffyrst at oᵣ londyng att Jaffe.

Sonday, the xij Day of Julii, that was relique Sonday, a bowt v of the Cloke at aftyr noon, we came to Jaffe, and fell to an

---

† Jeopardy.

Ankyr in the Rode ther. And in contynently we sent to Jheru-salem ffor the ffather Warden of the mounte Syon to com and se vs conducted to Jherusalem, As the custome ys.

Wedynsday, the xv Day of Julii, the ffather Warden of Bede-lem cam to vs with lordis of Jherusalem—And Rama thane beyng turkys—The great Turke havyng in Dominyon All the holl londe, And in shorte tyme they concludyd what sume ower patrone should pay for or tribute. And thanne we war suffered to com on londe.

The same Day at iij of Cloke at aftir noon, we com on londe, And as we came owt of the boott we war receyvyd by the Turkys and Sarrasyns, and put in to an old Cave by name and tale, ther Screvener ever wrytyng ower namys man by man As we entyred in the presens of the seyd lordis, And ther we lay in the same Grotte or cave all nyght upon the stynking Stable grounde, as well nyght as Day, ryght evyll intretyd by the seyd Turkes Mames.*

At this Jaffe begynnyth the holy londe, and to every pylgryme at the ffyrst foote that he set on the londe ther ys grauntyd plenary remission, De Pena et a Culpa.

At thys haven Jonas the prophete toke the see, whanne he fledde from the sithe of our lord in Tharsis.

---

* Our diarist applies several names to Turkish soldiers, as Moors, Mamelukes, Saracens, etc. Moors, though it might not be thought at first sight, is derived from the Arabic *gharb*, the west. Mameluke, or Memlook, is a white male slave. *Mames* is probably a mistake of the copier, and should be Maures.

And in the same Jaff, Seynt Petir reysid ffrom Deth Tabitam, the servaunt of the Appostolis. And fast by ys the place where Seynt Petir vsyd to ffyssh, And our Savior Crist Calleyd hym and seyd, sequere me.

This Jaff was Sumtyme a grett Citee, as it appereth by the Ruyne of the same, but nowe ther standeth never an howse but oonly ij towers, And Certeyne Caves vnder the grounde. And it was oon of the fyrst Cityes of the world ffounde by Japheth, Noes sonne, and bereth yett hys name.

Thursday, the xvj Day of Julii, at iiij of the Cloke at aftyr noone, we toke 3 assis and rode to Rama the same nyght, And ther we war Recyvyd into Duke Philipps hospitall. And it ys callyd so be cause Duke Philipp of Burgone, byldyd it of hys grett Charitie to Receye Pylgryms therin. We ffound no thyng therin, but bar walles and bar florethes, excepte oonly a well of good ffresh watir which was myche to our Comforth.

Nevtheles ther com to vs Jacobyns and other feynyd Cristen Peple of Sonndry Sectis, that browght to vs mattes ffor our mony to lye upon, And also brede, Sodying egges and sumtyme other vetaylles as mylke Grapys, and Appyllys. And ther we taryed all that nyght And ffriday all Day.

A bowt ij myle from Rama ys the Towne of Lydia, wher Seynt George suffered martydom and was hedyd. And in the same Seynt Peter helyd Enea of the Palsey. Rama ys from Jaff x myles, And from Jherusalem xxx myle, And vpon the right honde goyng ffrom Rama to Jherusalem a bowxt xx myle ffrom Rama ys the Castell of Emaus wher ij Discpulis of our Criste knew hym in brekyng of bred aftyr his Resurrecion as it ys well knowen by the Gospell.

A lytyll from thens, upon an hill called Mounte Joye, lyeth Samuell the Pphete. And a lityll ther by ys the towne of Ramathe where Samuell was born. And of thys towne was Joseph of Aramathia that awght the new Tumbe or Monyment that our Savir Crist was buryed in. And a lytyll over the myd way on the left honde ys the vale Terebynthy wher David overcome Goleam.

ffriday, the xvij Day of Julii, a bowte vj of the Cloke att aftyr noon the Turke, compellyd vs to com owt of our hospytall at Ramys, led vs in to the feld a myle with owt the Cetee where stondeth ij Towers, And ther we lay in the field all night.

Satirday, erley in the mornyng, we toke our Jorneyne towardys Jherusalem, And a bowt noon we restyd vs vndernethe the Olyff trees And ther refresshyd vs with Such mete ond wyne as we browght with vs from ower Shippe.

And a bowght vj or vij of the Cloke at after noon we cam to Jherusalem and were receyvyd into the Mounte Syon, And ther we supped, And aftyr Supper we war lede to our hospytall callyd Sancto Jacobo, ryght in the way to the holy Sepulcre Warde.

Sunday, the xix Day of Julii, we cam all to Mounte Syon to Masse, which was song ther ryght Devowtly. And thanne the Delyved to every Pylgryme a candyll of wax brennyng in his honde All the masse tyme, ffor which Candyll they recyvyd of every Pylgryme v gale ob.*

And whanne Masse was Don we went all to Dyn in the place wher we War ryght honestely svyed.†

And at medys of the Dyner the ffather Wardyn made a ryght holy sermon, and shewyd ryght Devoutly the holynesse of all the blyssyd choseyn place of the holy londe, And exortyd every man to cofession and repentaunce, And so to visite the seyd holy placis in clennes of lyff. And with shuch Devocion as all myghty god wold geff vnto them of hys most Speciall grace.

And thys Sermon Don, the ffader warden gaff vs warnyng that every man shuld provyd mete for him self and he wold fynd vs wyne, and so he Dede all the tyme that we war ther. And Carpetts to lay upon vs ffor the which every man pylgryme recompenssyd the seyd ffryers at ther Devocion.

As for bred and othe vitallys was broght to us for ower mony by persons of Divse sects. And all way the Wardeyne of the seyd ffrers or sum of hys Brothern by hys assigment Daly accompanyd with vs Informyng And shewing vnto vs the holy places with in the holy lande.

Munday, Seynt Margaretes Day, we begane ower Pylgrymage at the Mount Syon.

---

* Five Genoese " galleys," a small copper coin, value about ¼d., current in many parts of the Mediterranean owing to the scarcity of copper money and the extensive trade of the Genoese.

† Served.

ffyste the place wher the Jewys wold a restyd and take a way the holy body of our blyssyd lady whanne the Apostys bar hyr to the Vale of Josaphat to be buryed.

And ther by we cam in to a place wher Seynt Petir, Aftyr that he had Denyed our lord, thryse went owt of the howse of Cayphas in to a Cave and wept byttyrly, Whanne he hard the Coke crow iijes. The place ys callyd Gallicantus.

Pylgrmagis in to the Vale of Josophat.

And Thanne we Descendyd Downe by the Vale of Salamons temple. And fyrst we cam to Torrens Cedron, which in somer tyme ys Drye, And in wynter, and specially in lente, it ys mervelows flowyng with rage of watir that comyth with Grett violence thorow the vale of Josophat. And it renne be twyne the Citee and the Mounte of Olivete, And it ys callyd as it ys be for Torrens Cedron. And over the same watir seynt Eline made a brygge of stone whiche ys yett ther over. And many yers be for the passion of Crist, the lay over the same watir a tree, ffor a foote bryge, wheroff the holy Crosse was aftyr wardes made. This seying Quene Saba, by the spirite of prophecie, whanne she passyd that wey she wold nott trede thervpon, but wadyd thorow the watir. Seying that the Savyor of all the world shuld suffre hys Deth vpon that Tree, Ther is clene remission.

And thus Descendyd we come to the botome of the Vale of Josophat and begynnyth the Vale of Siloe, And they both be but on vale, but the name Chaungeth. And att the bygynyng of thys Vale ys a fayer Tombe in the maner of a tower substancially made, Wherin as ys sayd Absolon ys buryed. And so ever ony Sarazin comyth by that Sepulcre he cast a stonne ther att with grett violence and Dispite, by cause the seyd Absolon pursued hys father, king David, and cause hym to flee.

And sum other men Say it ys the sepulcre of Josophat, And that the Vale take the name of the seyd Josophat.

Nott far from thys place ys the myddys of the vale of Josophate, wher ys a very fayer churche in the kepyng and handys of the Sarazyns, wherin we Descendid in to a wonde ffayer vawght by xlviii grees.* Wher ys the holy Tombe of our blyssyd lady, wher she was buryed by the Apostoles, And aftyr that Assumpte in to hevyn. And ther ys clene remission.

Pylgrymages at the Mounte of Olivete.

Departyng owt of thys forseyd churche of ower lady, we Came to the fote of the Mounte of Olyvete, And a lytyll Ascendyng we came to the place vnder an holow Roke, wher our savyor preying fell in such an Agony that he Swete watir and blode That the Droppes ffell in grett plenty from hys eyne to the erthe, seying, Pater si possibile est vt transseat a me calix iste verumtamen, non sicut ego volo sed sicut tu vis ffiat voluntas tua. Clene remission.

Ther is Also the stone wher vpon the Aungell stod comfortyng hym the same tyme.

ffrom thens Descendyng a stonys Cast we came to the place

---

* A wondrous fair vault by 48 steps.

wher our savyor Crist left Petir, Jamis, and John. Sedete hic Donec vadam illuc et orem. vigilate et orate.

ffrom thens we assendyd in to the place wher as Seynt Thomas the Apostill receyved the Gyrdyll of our lady whanne she was Assumpte.

. ffrom thense we entred in to the gardeyn and visited the place wher our savyor was takyn and where Seynt Petir Stroke of Malcus eere.

And therby ys the place shewyd by a token of a ston wher Judas be trayed our Savyor to the Jewys with a kysse, And wher the Jewis fell bakward, when Crist seyd, Quem queritis, Illi autem Dixerunt Jhm nazarenum. And yet we ascendid mor and came to the place wher ower Savyor Crist seying and be holdyng the Citie of Jherusalem vpon Palme of Sonnday wepte vpon seing, Si cognovisses et tu, S. fleres, etc.

ffrom thens we Ascendid mor hyer and come to a place wher the Aungell of ower lord browght a palm vnto our blyssyd lady shewying vnto hyr the Day of hyr Dethe.

Also thanne we cam to the place wher our blyssyd lady Dede reste hyr many tymes ffor werynesse whanne she went pylgrmagis aftyr the passion of our lorde, And also hys assencion.

Also wher the Postyllys * made Crede of ower feyth.

Also a lityll thense ys the place wher ower Savyor Crist

---

* Apostles.

taught hys Discipulis to pray, Seying Cum oratis ita Dicite Pater noster.

Thanne next we went vnto the hyethe and tope of thys seyd Mounte of Olivete, wher we founde an olde Chirche with ine the whiche Chrche ys a fayer Tower xiij Sqware, And on the on Syde ys a Dore, And in the myddys of the Tower ys the place wher our blyssyd Savyor Crist Jhu ascendid vnto hevyn. Videntibus illis, etc.

In the same Tower ys the ston vpon the whiche ower Savyor stonding ascendid in to hevyn, in the whiche stone The prynte Of hys holy foote yett appere, And specially of the ryght foote. Ther ys clene remission.

And from thense we Ascendid a lytyll And come to a nother tower Callyd Galilee and that ys the Place of the whiche the Aungell shewyng the resurrection of our Savyor, seyd to ys Discipulis, Precedet vos in Galileam ibi eum videbitis sicut predixit vobis. Accordyng to the promyse of our Savyor made a for hys passion, whanne he seyd Postquam Resurrexero precedam vos in Galileam. That ys for to sey into the seyd Place Callyd Galilee. And not in to the Region of Galilee whiche ys ffer from thys place.

And whanne we war on the mounte of Olivete we myghte se pfyghtly, Vpon the Golden gate of the temple of Salomon, of whiche gate or lord rode in on Palme Sonnday. But no Cristen man ys not suffered for to come ny it.

Neverthelesse to them that with Devocion behold it a ffar ys grauntyd clene remission.

Thanne we Descendyng the same way that ower lorde rode vpon palme Sonnday, And cam to the Place wher the Chyldern of Israell brake braunches of Olyff trees and kest in the way a ffor ower Savyor whanne he rode on hys Asse towards Jherusalem, And they songe, Osanna Benedictus qui venit in nomine domini.

And thanne be the ledyng and conductyng of ower seyd gydes we decenddid in to the Vale of Josophat, but not the same wey we went owte warde. Ther we Ascendid vp to the gate of the Citee callyd Seynt Stevyns gate, ffor ther ys the Place wher Seynt Stephen was stoyned to Deth, And wher Saule stod and kepte hys clothes with in Jherusalem.

And a non we entred in att the forseyd gate, and on the left hande with in the gate ys Probatica Piscina vnder the wale of the Temple of Salomon, in the whiche Place ower lord shewyd many Miraclis as it ys well knowen by the Gospell.

ffrom thence we went to the howse wher the Synnys of Mary Mawdleyn war for govyn.

Therby ys an other howse that sumtyme was a fayer Churche of Seynt Anne. But now the Sarrasyns have made ther of a muskey,* that is for to sey ther Temple. And that ys the self Place that was Seynt Annes howse. And ther She Deyed. And in a vawght vnderneth ys the very self Place wher our blyssyd lady was born. And ther ys Plenarie Remission.

---

* Mosque.

The stonys of that Place wher ower lady was born ys remedi and consolacion to women that Travell of Chylde.

ffrom thense we went to the howse of Herode, that ys on the left hande of Pylates howse. And stondyth heyer vpon the ffronte of the hyll. In to the whiche howse ower Savyor was presentyd vnto herodes by Pylates sendyng acusyd by the Jewys neverthelesse. The seyd herode Clothed hym in a white Garment and sent hym agen to Pilate, Et facti sunt Amici herodes et Pilatus in illo Die, etc. And ij howses of Pilate and Herode be yet now the fayrest howses in Jherusalem, and specially the howse of king Herode.

Item. As we passyd by the strete ther stondeth An arche ov the way, vpon the which stondyth ij large whitht stonys. Vpon the oon of them our Savyor stode whanne he was jugede to Deth, And on the other stone stode Pylate whanne he gaff Sentence that he shuld be Crucyfyed.

The next place that we cam ys wher ower blyssyd lady stode whanne she mette with hyr Der sonne beryng his Crosse, wher for over myche Sorow and Dolor of harte She Sodenly fell in to a sowne and forgetfullnesse of hyr mynde, and thys holy Place ys callyd Sancta Maria De Spasimo. Seynt Elyne byldyd a chirche ther, but yt ys Downe. And the Sarrazins have often attempted to bylde ther, but ther edifying wold not stonde in no wyse.

Item, the next place ys wher the Jewes Constrayned Symeon Cirenen, commyng from the Towne, to take the Crosse and ber it aftyr our Savyor Criste.

And from thense we went to a place callyd Bivium, that ys as myche for to sey as a Crosse strete or a Crosse wey, wher the women of Jherusalem stod and Sorowfully wepte whanne our lord was lede to hys Deth, To whom he seyd wepe ye nott vpon me ye Doughters of Jherusalem, But wepe ye vpon yower self and vpon yower Chyldern.

And from thense we went to the howse of Dives Epulonis qui Sepultus est in Inferno.

And fyrst, as our wey lay, we cam to the howse of Veronica, whych ys from the howse of Pilate vcl pace, wher as our blyssid Savyor impressyd the ymage of hys fface in hyr wymple whiche ys at Rome. And it ys callyd ther the Vernacle.

And so we visited all the long wey by which our Savyor Criste was lede from the howse of Pilate vnto the place of hys Cruci-fying.

And also we passyd by the gate of the Temple of the holy Sepulcre, and in ower wey homward we cam to the Chirche that the Jacobyns hold. In the chirche syd ys a lytyll Chapell in the whiche Chapell Seynt Jamis the mor* was hedyd by king herode.

Also therby ys the place wher our lord Criste aftyr hys Resur-recion apperyd To mary Mawdleyn and to other Devowte women in the hye wey as they com from hys Sepulcre, wher he seyd on to them. Avete, And ther with they com ner hym, Et tenuerunt pedes eius.

---

* St. James the More, or Great.

F

And all theses Stacions thus visited the Day of Seynt Margarete afore rehersyd. We returnyd to the Mounte Syon to reffressh us and ther restyd us for a Certeyn tyme.

Pylgrimage of the Mownte Syon.

A lityll from the Movnte Syon, The Chirche of the Aungellis, wher sumtyme was the howse of Annas the Busshope, in to the which our Savior Criste was ffyrst lede ffrom the Mownte of Olivete, wher he sufferyd many Iniuris. And specially ther he toke a buffet of on of the busshopps servaunts, Seying, Sic respondes Pontifici.

ffrom thense we went to a Chirche of Seynt Savior, wher sum tyme stod the grett hous of Chayphas wher our blyssyd Savior was scornyd, hys face Coverd and bobbyd,* And most grevowsly betyn and ther sufferyd many afflicions all that nyght. Ther ys allso a lytyll cave at the Auters ende wher they shette hym ynne tyll the Jewys had taken ther counsell and Determynyd what they wold Do with hym. And it ys yett callyd Carcer Dni.

Ther ys also in the same place the moste parte of the grett stonne that the Aungell as we rede Removyd ffrom the Dor of the Sepulcre. And it is now the stone of the hye auter in the same Churche. And the other parte of the Same stone lith yett beffore the Sepulcre Dore.

And ther with owt the Door in the Courte, on the left honde, ys a tree with many stonys a bowght it, wher the ministres of the Jewys

---

* Befooled, or mocked.

and Seynt Petir with them warmyd them by the ffyer. And goyng owt of the same Courte, in the hygh wey on the ryght honde, in a Corner, ys astone wher our blyssyd lady stode whanne Petir went owt Sore wepyng. And hys wepying was so myche that he cowd not geff hyr non Answer whanne she inquired of hyr Swete sonne. And ther she Desyrows to know of hyr sonne, Most Sorrowfull a bode tyll in the mornyng That She saw them lede hym bownde to the howse of Pilate, whethir she most Sorowfully folowyd hym.

A lityll from thys Chirche ther appeareth a Ruyne of an old falyn Chirche wher thys most glorius virgine, aftyr the Deth of our Savyor hyr sonne, Dwellyd and bode most Devowtly by the space of xiiij yerys vn to the Day of hyr Assumption. And ther ys clene remission.

Ther by ys the place and a stone lying wher our blyssyd lady Died and assumptyd In to hevyn. Ther ys clene Remission.

Ther by Also ys a parte of a stone upon the whych Seynt John Evngeliste sayd often Masse be fore that blyssyd lady as her Chapleyn aftyr the assencion of ower lorde.

Ther ys Also the place shewyd by a stonne whiche ys a yard of hight, wher Seynt Mathe was Chosyn in to the Nowmber of the Apostolys.

ffrom thens going in to the Mownte Syon, fast by the Chirche, ys the place wher our blyssyd lady vsyd to sey hyr most Devowte Prayers and Dayly Devowte Devocions at the Assencon of our lord and be for.

Also therby be ij stonys, upon oon of them ower Savyr Criste vsed to sitt and preche to hys Discipls, And upon the other satt hys blyssed mother heryng hys seyd prechynges.

Under the Chirche of the seyd Syon ys the Sepulcre or byryall of prophets and kyngs of Israell. As David, Salomon, Roboas Abias, Asa, Jeconias, Sedechias, with many moo. In thys Sepultur ys no Cristen man suffred to entre, ffor the Sarrazins kepte that Place in grett revence and worshippe it ryght myche in ther maner, and have made ther of ther muskey. That ys for to sey ther Chirche or Chapell.

Ther by ys the place wher Seynt Stevin the ij^de tyme Seynt Gamaliell, Seint Poules techer, Abbibas his sonne, And Nichodem war buryed.

Also therby ys the place wher the Pascall lambe was rostyd, etc. And wher the watir was hett* to wassh the ffete of Cristis Discipulis.

And Ther fast by ys the Place wher kyng David Dyd penaunce, and made the vij Psalmys for the sleyng of Vrye,† whom he put in the forh frontt of the batell porposly to have hym slayne to the entent that he myght the mor at liberte vse hys wyff whom he kept in advoutre.

The Pylgimagis w^t in the Place of Mownte Syon.

ffyrst in the sayd Chirche of Mownte Syon, in the self place wher the hyeh auter ys, Ower blyssyd Savior Crist Jhu made hys

---

* Heated ?   † Uriah.

last Soper and mawdy* wt his Discipulis, And made ther the Preciose Sacrament of hys blyssyd body that we vse Dayly in memory of hys glorius passion. Ther ys clene remission.

And vpon the ryght honde of the seyd hyeh Auter ys a nother Auter in the next yle, wher our Savyor wasshed hys Discipullys ffete at the seyd Mawndy.

Also a loft wythowt forth at the queres end, ys the place wher the holy goost com and Discendid vpon hys Discipulis in the likenesse of brennyg tongis, and in spiryd them vpon whithsonday, as the Servyce of same ffest shewyth. And ther ys clene Remyssion.

And vnder nethe in the Cloyster in the same place, ys a lytyll Chapell wher our Savyor Crist aftyr hys Resurreccon apperyd to hys Discipulis, the Dorys shete, And aftyr viij Days, whanne they war a geyn gaderyd to gedyr, And Seynt Thomas with them, he cam vpon them agen, and seyd to Thomas, Infer Digitum tuum et mitte manum tuam in latus meum, etc. Clene remission.

Thys Citie of Jherusalem ys a ffayer Emynent Place, for it stondith vpon suche a grounde, That from whens so ever a man comyth ther he must nedys ascende.

ffrom thens a man may se all Arabye, And the Mownte of Abaryn, and Nebo, and Phasga, the playnes of Jordan, And Jherico, And the Dede see vnto the ston of Deserte. I saw never

---

* Maunday, Holy Thursday.

Citie nor other place have so fayer prospects. It stondeth fayer a mong hyllys and ther ys no Ryver comyng ther to, nor well in it, but the watir cometh all by condite, in grett plente, ffrom Ebrom* and Bedelem, which condites serve all the Citee in every place, And fyll all the pyscynes, whiche are in grett nowmber, And myche watir renneth now to waste.

Thys londe of Jherusalem hath ben in the handys of many Sundry Nacions. As of Jewys, Cananers, Asseryens, Parciens, Macidens, Medoyns, Grekes, Cristen Men, Sarrasyns, Barbaryns, Turkes, and many other nacions.

Jherusalem ys in the londe of Jude, and it marcheth Estwardis to the kyngdom of Araby, Southwardys to the londe of Egipte, of Westward to the grett see, Northwardis to the kingdom of Surr, † And to the se of Cipres, in sum place. And the seyd holy lond ys in length, North and Suth, ix score myle, And in bred, Est and west, lx myle.

Pylgrimages with ine the Temple of the holy Sepulcre.

The Tewysday, at vj of the cloke at aftyr non, that was the evyn of Seynt Mari Mawdleyn, we war admitted by the lordes, Turkes, and Mamolukes of the Citie, to entre in to the Temple of the holy Sepulcre, Dilyvd in by them by name and tale, And at the seyd entre to every pylgryme ys granted plenary remission, De pena et a culpa.

---

* Hebron. † Syria.

The same tyme the moste parte of the ffryers of the Mownte Syon Entred with us in to the seyd temple, ffor they have certeyn placys in ther kepyng with in the same, That ys for to sey the holy Sepulcre. And the Chapell of our lady wher our savyor apperyd fyrst on to her aftyr hys resurreccon, And Sayd Salve sancta parens, wherin be contynually at the leste ij ffryers of the seyd mownte Sion, to kepte Devowtly the seyd holy places, and ther lyvyng ys mynystired vnto them twyes a Day from the seyd Mownte Syon. And ye shall vnderstonde that the Doores of the seyd Temple of the Sepulcre be never openyd by the paynyms, But by the commyng of Pylgrymys at ther grette Sute and Coste, or to chaunge ffryers that have the kepyng of the seyd places with in the Temple.

And over thys ye shall vnderstonde that ther be in Jheruslm ix Diverses Sectis of Cristen men. And every of the have places Distincte and severall to them self with in the Temple of the holy Sepulcre, to vse the ryghte of ther Sectis, And with owt forth be for the Entre into thys Temple x pacis in Distan ys put a ston in memory and token that our Savior Crist beryng hys Crost for very febylnesse fell ther to the grounde vnder nethe Crosse.

The Chirche of the holy Sepulcre ys Rounde, myche leke the forme and makyng of the Temple at London,* saff it ys excedyng fer in gretnesse, and hath wonder many yles, Crodes† and vowtes, Chapellys hygh and lowe, in grett nowmber, and mervell it ys

---

* The round church of the Temple still existing.
† Crowds, choirs, or corridors.

to see the many Deferens and secrete places with in the sayd temple. And the grett gounde parte westwarde of the seyd tempe ys all open in the Roffe, wher vnder stondith the holy sepulcre of our lord, whiche ys made all of ston Rooke, And all in forme of a lytyll Capell. And fyrst at the entre of the same ys a lytyll Door, wher we come into a lytyll rounde Chapell ꝼ vowtyd, other wyse callyd a spelunke,* of viij foote of brede and as myche in length. And from thys we entred into a myche lesse, and a lower Doore, And come in a like spelunke. And vpon the ryht hande of the same, evyn with ine the seyd low Door, ys the very holy Sepulcre of our lord cov with a mervyll stone the lenght wher of ys viij foote. And ther ys no light in to the seyd lytyll Spelunke of the Sepulcre by no manere of wyndow, But the lyght ys ther mynystred by many lampes hangyng within the seyd Spelunke ov the Sepulcre.

In to the ffyrst of thes ij Spelunks entred the women whanne they seyd, Quis revolvit nobis lipidem ab hostio† monumenti And parte of the same stone lieth ther yett now in the same vttermost Spelunk, And the other grettest parte ys a stonne of the hye Auter, in Seynt Savyor Churche, wher of ys mencion made by for.

Off the procession Doon ther.

Tewysday, that was Seynt Mary Mawlyn evyn, at vj of the cloke at aftyr none, we entred in to the holy sepulcre. Thanne war we had by and by in to the Chapell of ower blyssyd lady,

---

* Latin, spelunca, a cave.   † Ostio, St. Mark xvi. 3.

whiche the ffryers kepte and ther thei made the redy in ornaments And be gan ther a very solempne procession. And at every Stacion was shewyd vn to vs by on of the ffryers, the mysterys and holynesse of the places wher they made ther Stacions. And thei sang Antemes, ympnys versiculis, and collects approperyd on to the seyd holy place ryght Solennly and Devowtly. And ffyrst at the procedyng owt of the seyd Chapell of ower blyssyd lady, They Shewyd on to vs that ther the hye Auter ys of the same Chapell, ys the very self place wher our Savyor Crist aftyr hys Resurreccion ffyrst apperyd vnto hys blyssyd mother, And seyd, Salve Sancta Parens. And ther ys plenary remission.

Also in the same Capell, on the ryght honde of the seyd high Auter, with in a vowte, in maner of a wyndow, ys a grett pece of the peler that our Savyor was bound to whanne in the Howse of Pilate.

Also in the same Chapell, vpon the left honde of the seyd hye Auter, in a lyke wyndow, ys the place where longe remayned the holy Crosse of ower Savyor Criste, aftyr that Seynt Elyne fond it, and now ther remayne non of it.

Also in the myddes of that Chapell ys the Place wher the holy crosse was provyd by resyng of a Dede man whanne they wer in Dowte whiche it was of the thre.

Thys Day the procession procedyd forthe and we folowyd with prayers and contemplacion as Devowtly as all myghty god yaff vs grace with Candyllys of wax brennyng in our handys.

And goyng owt of the seyd Chapell, with owt the Dore of the

same, be ij whith marble stonys round a bowte x foote a sundre
the on ys the place wher ower Savyr stode whanne he apperyd to
Mary mawdeleyn aftyr hys Resurreccon, in lekeness of a gard-
ner. And the other ston ys the place wher Mary mawdeleyn
stode and Seyd, Raboni. Thanne our Savyor Criste seyd, Maria
noli flere. And thanne she knew hym perfyghtly.

ffrom thense we Descendid in to a corner of an yle of the same
Chirche, wher ys a lityll vowght, Strongly made, wherin owyr
Savyr was kept in preson, whiles hys Crosse was in Dressyng
and makyn redy.

Also next thys place ys an Auter wher the Crucyfyers Devydyd
hys Clothes by Chaunce of the Dyce.

ffrom thens we Discendyd in to a lowe Chapell by xxx grees,
wher Seynt Elyn Stode, Sawe, and commaundyd the Diggyng of
the Invencion of the holy Crosse. And aftyr warde she made
ther hyr Oratry, And vsyd to sey her Devocions and prayers
most comonly in the same palce.*

In the same Chapell at the Auters ende, on the Right hande,
ys a wyndow, wher, aftyr messe, Seynt Elyn vsyd to knele and
wepe by the space of half an howre, ffor ther she see the place
wher she fonde the most holy Crosse perfyghtyly. And ther ys
clene remisson.

ffrom thense we Discendid by xj grees, that browght vs in to
a place vnder a Rooke, xxij fote of brede, wher the holy Crosse,

---

* Sic in MS.

the Spere, the Nayles, and the Crowne of Thorne of our blyssyd Savyor war founde, whiche place ys spoke by for. And ther ys Also clene remission.

Also from thense we ascendid a gen in to the Churche, and came to an Auter, vnder the whych ys a place of stone myche lyke a pece of a pyler, vpon the whyche our Savyor Sate in the Courte of Pilate whanne he was Crowned with thornys, Scornyd and buffetyd.

ffrom thense we ascendyd by xviij grees, and cam to the Mownte of Calvery, wher o^r Savyor Crist was Crucyfyed and suffered Deth for ower redempcon, and ther ys a fayer large Chapell, well vowted, and lytyd by many lampes brennyng, this place ys mervelows holy and venerable a bove all other.

Also vpon the hight of the same Mownte of Calvery, ys the very hold or morteys hevyn owt of the stone Rooke wherin the Crosse stode, with ower blyssyd Savyor at the tyme of hys passion, whyche Morteys ys in Depnesse ij Spannys to the botom, the brede ys sumwhat more thane a Spanne. And ther ys a plate of Coper Sett with inne the compas of the Stone to the entent that no man shuld kutt nor take a wey any parte of the Sayd ston, and soo Disfygur the same Morteys.

Therby Also by the space of viij palmes from the place of the left Arme of Crist hanging on the Crosse ys a scissur or clyfte in the Stone Rooke so myche that a man may almost lye therine, whiche Ryft goth Downe thorow the rokke of Calvery and appereth by nethe at the Pavyment of the nether Chapell and so goth thorow owt the erthe, vsque in abissu, whiche Clyft with moo ther be but not so myche Reffe at the precious Dethe of our Savyor Crist.

And it ys of a trouthe as they sey ther, And it ys assigned by token of a fayer ston layde for remembrance that ower blyssyd lady and Seynt John Evngeliste stod not a bove upon the hyest parte of the mounte of Calvery at the passion of our lord, as it ys poyntyd And kerven* in many places, But she stod sumwhat benethe by for hyr Der sonne face to face at the tyme of hys precious Deth.

Vnder the mounte of Clavery ys another Chapell of our blyssyd lady and Seynt John Evngeliste that was callyd Galgatha, and ther, ryght vnder the Morteys of the Crosse, was founde the hede of our fore father Adam.

ffrom the Mownte of Calvery we Decendyd and cam to the place assigned like a grave, wher ower blyssyd lady most Dolorous mother Satt havyng in hyr lappe the Dede body of hyr Dere sone, new takeyn Downe from the Crosse, to be put in hys Sepulcre, Seynt John Evngeliste knelyng by her, And Seynt Mari Mawleyn knelyng at our lordys feete.

ffrom thens we went and made our stacion at the holy Sepulcre, as in to the pryncipall of that Temple, ffor all the holl Temple ys Dedicate and halowed in the honor and name of the holy Sepulcre.

Off the whyche Sepulcre ys wrytyn more largely at the begynnyng of the Chaptre.

---

* Painted and carved.

And ffrom thys holy Sepulcre we went a gen, folowyng always the procession into the Chapell of our lady, wher as we fyrst be gan to go forth with the seyd procession, and ther we made an ende.

And whanne we war retornyd a yen on to the sayde Chapell of ower lady, aftyr a lytyll refeccion with mete and Drynke, evy man thanne gaff hym self to Prayer and contemplacion, besely visyng the holy places a for sayd aftyr ther Devocion. Duryng the hole nyght And erly in the mornyng, all we that war prestis seyd messe, Sum at Calvery, Sum at ower ladys Chapell, And Sum At the holy Sepulcre aftyr our Devocion. And the laye Pylgrmes war howsyld* at the Chapell of Calvery.

And also by vij or viij of the cloke in the mornyng we had seyd all messe. And thanne We refreshed vs with wyne and bred and such other caseles as we cowd gett for ower mony of the Thurkes And Sarrasyns.

The same wedynsday that was the Day of mary Mawdleyn, we taryd all Day and all nyght in the Temple of the holy Sepulcre. And the next morow we sayd masse as we Ded the tewysday be for.

Thursday, that was the xxiij Day of Julii, a bowth x or xj of the cloke, the Gatys of the holy Temple of the Sepulcre war Sett opyn And thanne we went all to the Mownte Syon to Dyner.

And so it appereth that we war in the Temple of the holy

---

* Received the Holy Sacrament.

Sepulcre ij Dayes and ij nyghts, And never com owte the for seyd tyme.

The same Thursday at aftyr noon we toke our assys at the Mownte Syon, accompanyed with the seyd ffreres and Turkes and rode the same nyght to Bethlem whiche ys v myle for Jherusalem.

And in the high way by twyne, a bowte ij myle from Jherusalem, we com to a place wher the starre appered ageyn to the iij kynges, wherof they lost ther light at ther entre into Jherusalem wherby they rode forthe to Jherusalem.

And a lytyll forther we com to a old Chirche, wher the prophete Elias was born.

And ther by ys a place wher the Aungell toke vp Abacok by the fronte And bar hym to Babylon and sett hym in the lake of lyons wher Danyell the pphete was, and refresshed hym with mete and Drynke.

Nott far thens we myght se the place in which Jacobb the patriarke, Dwellyd And ther also we passyd fast by the Sepulcre of Rachell the wyff of the seyd Jacobe.

Thanne next we cam to Bethelem, it was callyd in old tyme Effrata, wherof it ys wretyng Ecce Audivimus eum in effrata.

A lytyll withowt the same Citie, towardys the Est, ys the fayer chirche of ower blyssyd lady, wher ower Savyr Criste was born, wherof shalbe made more mencion aftyrward.

And bytwyne Citie and the seyd Chirche ys the flod floridus

where the fayer mayd shuld a ben brent.* And was Savyd harmlesse by myracle, for the fyer chaunged in to Rosis. And in thys Citie of Bethelem was kyng David born.

The same thursday as we cam to thys Bethelem, and a lytyd at the Chirche of our lady a forsayd, whych ys a mervelus fayer Chirche and a rygth Sumptuos werke, the length therof ys ccxxviij fote, And the bred ys lxxxvij fote. Ther be iiij rowes or Ranges of pylers thorow the Chirche.

The Sawdon† was in porpuse to a removyd those pyllers, and to a caryed them to have byldyd hys paleys with the same. And for that intent he can to Bethlem in hys owne persone to se them take Downe. And he be held the Masons begynnyng to breke. So Deuly ther came owt of the Chirche wall with in forth ny ther the Sowdon was, an howge gret Serpent that ranne endlong vpon the ryght Syde of the Chirche wall, and scorged the seyd wall as it had be sengid with fyer all the wey that he wente, whyche schorchyng ys sene in to thys Day.

And with thys sygn the Sawdon a voydyd with grett fere, And all tho that war with hym, And nev sythyns he nor non other attempted to remove ony thyng ther.

At Bethelem, comonly be v or vj friers of Mowte Syon, to kepe the holy place ther, whiche with other fryers that cam with us to Mownte Syon, Dressed them to solempne procession at our fyrst

---

* I have entirely failed to find this story : but several more or less like it are in the *Legenda Sanctorum.*

† Sultan.

commyng, whome we folowyd to all the holy placys with in the same Monasteri, with candels light in ower handys, as all wey vsyd in other place wher ony procession was Don.

And fyrst the seyd procession browght vs to a place at an Aulter in the suth yle wher our Savyr Crist was Circumsysed.

And from thens we came to an other Auter on the Northe syd, wher the iij kyngs made redy ther offeryngs to present on to ower Savor Criste.

And from thys place, Descendyng certayne grees of stone, we com in to a wonder fayer lityll Chapell, at the hyer auter wherof, ys the vary place of the byrth of our lord, Assigned by a sterre made in a fayer whith marble stone. Vnder the myddys of the seyd high Auter, whych byrth was Don in the self most holy place to the gretest Joy and gladnesse that ever cam to mankynde.   And at thys holy place ys clene Remission.

And ther by ys a lityll Auter sum what vnder the Rook, wher the iij kyngs offered to ower blyssyd Savyor Criste Jhu, Gold, Myrre, and Incence, and ther ys clene remission.

And a lityll be for the seyd Aulter ys the Cribbe of our lord, wher ower blyssyd lady leyd hyr Dere sone be for hyr, The oxe and the Asse. clene Remission.

And vndowtyd thys lityll Chapell of the byrthe of ower lord ys the most glorius and Devowte place that ys in the world, Somyche thot that excedith in holynesse all other places that be in this worlde.

It ys Also of tables of fyne whith marble stonne. And the vowtys be garnyshyd with gold and byse* with Diverse Storys of a substyll musyk† werke as may be. The walles also of all the body of the Chirche, from the pyllers to the Rooff, be poyntyd with storys from the begynnyng of the world of the same musyng werkys, whyche ys the Richeest thyng that canne be Don to any wallis.

How be it the seyd werkes be gretly Defauncyd, bothe in the Chirche and in the Chapell, for very pure Age, And the seyd Churche wyth all the places falleth in gret Dekay.

And whanne we had vysyted thys holy Chapell, we ascendid, and come to the place wher the bodys of the holy Innocets lay many yers vnknowen.

Item, fast by the same Chapell, ys a nother lityll Chapell, wher Seynt Jherom was buryd, and ther ys yet hys tombe, but hys body was translat to Rome long Syns.

Ther ys also another solytary Chapell vnder a Rooke, wher Seynt Jherom translated the bybyll in to Greke and latyn.

Thys procession ended, we refressyd vs with such vitallys as we had and restyd vs a while, And that Day every man gaff hym to prayer and contemplacion, visityng the holy place a forseyd.

And aftyr myde night, seying and hering messis vnto the tyme it was Dailyght, At which tyme the Chirche Dores war sett

---

* Beset.   † Mosaic.

G

open by the Paynymys, by whom we war let owt, by tale, as we entred in, And thanne we visited the holy place a bowte Bethlem.

ffyrst the place wher the Aungell of god apperyd to Joseph in hys Slepe, Saying, Surge et accipe puerum et matrem eius et fuge in Egiptum.

At the Est ende of the Chirche of Bethlem ys A cave in the grounde, wher sumtyme stod a Chirch of Seynt Nicholas. In the same Cave Entred ower blyssid lady with hyr Sone, And hyd hyr, for ffer of kyng Herrod, the gronde ys good for Norces, that lake mylk for ther Childern.

Ther ys a nother place wher Sumtyme stod a Chirche of our lady, Distante from ower lady of Bethlem, v arrow shots, wher at the byrth of our lord The Aungell seyd on to the Shepperds, Anuncio vobis gaudium magnum Quia natus est hodie salvator mundi.

A lityll thense ys the place wher the herdmen kepte ther watche vpon ther flock, in the houre of the nativite of ower lord, Sawe and hard the Aungellis syng, Gloria in excelsis Deo. this place ys ij myle from Bethelem.

And thens, the same ffryday, that was the vigill of Seynt Jamis, we retornyd to Bethelem, to ower Dyner a geyne, and ther refresshed vs to the tyme it was paste noon.

Pylgrymage to ye mowntis of Jude.

A bowte ij of the cloke at Aftyr none, we toke our assis at Bethelem, ffyrst we come to the Sepulcre of the vij prophetis.

Ther ys also the place wher David Slew Golyas.

And from thense we com to the howse of Zacharie, in the Mowntayns of Jude whych ys v myle from Bethelem, and v from Jherusalem, in to the whiche howse of zacharie, aftyr the salutacon of the Aungell, and the conception of Crist, The most blyssyd virgine goyyng in to the Mowntaynes with grett spede, entred and salutyd Elisabeth, and mad thys Swete song, Magnificat anima mea Dmn.

And ther by was sumtyme a Chirche that nowe ys fallyn, wherys the place wher zacharie fulfyllyd with the holy gost prophesyd, Saying, Benedictus Dns Deus Israll, And wher he askyd pene and ynke, and wrotte hys sonne, Johes est nomen eius.

Thanne next aftyr we come to the howse of Symyonis Justi et Timorati, the whiche recevyd Criste in hys Armys, whanne he was presentyd in to the temple, seying, Nunc Dimittis Dne svu. tuu.

In ower way home wardys, ij myle from Jherusalem, we com vnto a cloyster of Grekkys monkes, whose chyrche ys of the holy crosse, etc., ther as the hye auter of the `same Chirche stondeth, ys the place wher the tree grew that the holy Crosse was made.

And ther by ys Salomons archezard,* whyche ys yett a Dilectable place.

---

* Orchard.

Thus we cam to Jherusalem, the same Satyrday, at nyght, and went to Mounte Syon, and ther refresshed vs and rested vs for that nyght.

SatyrDay, at aftyr noon, we visited places a bowyt Jherusalem, it was Seynt Jamys Day.

ffyrst we came to an old brokyn Castyll, where the Jewys wher gadererd to gedyr of a counsell at the tyme of the passion of our lord, and Judas went to counsell with them to the same place. And it ys callyd now malu. consilium.

ffrom thense we cam to Acheldemake, other wyse Callyd terra Sancta, that was bowght with the xxx pece of silver that our Savyor was sold for by Judas. And ther ys made a grett vowght, and ther be vij holes a bowght to cast the Dede Cristen mens bodyes in to the seyd vowght or cave, it was so ordeynyd and Dressyd by Seynt Elyn.

Ther by in the Rokkes be certayne Caves, wher the Apostolys hid them in the tyme of the passion of our lorde.

Item, not farr from thense we cam to a fayer tree, w^t a grett hepe of stonys a bowght it, wher Ysac, the pphete, was Sawen in sounder by the myddys w^t a sawe of Tree.

Ther ys also by Ortus Olerum, ther ronnys watyr properly in that Garden.

Than we cam to Natatorium Siloe, wher our Savyor gaff sight to the born blynde man, a noyntyng hys eyne with Claye and Spetyll, Saying, Vade, et lava in Natatoria Siloe Qui abiit et venit videns.

And aftyr that we cam to a ffountayne wher our blyssyd lady was wont many tymes to wasse hyr clothes, and the clothes of ower blyssyd Savyor in hys chyldhod.

ffrom thense we cam to the Chirche of Seynt Jamys the lesse, in a Cave wher he hyd hym the tyme of the passion of our lord, a vowyng that he wold never ete mete vnto the tyme he sawe hys Mayster Criste rysen vpon Estern Day. Erly in the mornyng ower blyssyd Savyr com to hym, and browght hym mete, saying, Jamis, now ete, for I am rysyn.

Item, ther by ys the Sepulcre of zacharie, the prophete. And from thense we com to the place wher sumtyme stode the Towne of Gethsemany, which is rehersyd in scriptur.

Thes places thus visited, we retorynd homwarde a geyne, be the Temple of Salomon, whiche ys callyd Porticus Salomonis. And ther we myght se grett nowber of lampes brennyng in the seyd Temple at the Sone sett.

And so we went to our hospitall and restyd vs for that nyght.

The same Sonday that Seynt Annys Day, a fore nòon, we went to Bethanye, whiche ys be yon the Mownte of Olyvete ij myle from Jherusalen. Ther we Entred in to an Old Chirche, And Sawe the grave or monument in the which Lazarus lay iiij Days Dede, as the Gospell sheweth, etc., whom our Savyor Crist reysyd from Deth to lyff.

Not far from theinse ys the house of Simonis leprosi, whiche preyd ower lorde to ete with hym. And ther as he Satt, Mary mawdleyn browght Alabauster of an onyment, and satt at our lordys fete, and with owt seassyng, whesshed hys fete with hyr terys, wppyng them with hyr her of hyr hede, And a noyntyd them with hyr precious onyment. And ther our Savyr for gaff the synnys of the sayd mary Mawdleyn.

Thys Symon leprosus that harborowed our lorde And suche of hys Disciplis as war Cristeyned, was aftyr warde made Bushoppe, And he was namyd Julian. And thys ys he that men call vpon for good harborowe.

Ther by ys the howse of the Martha, our lordes hostes, And the howse of the seyd Mary Mawdleyn, whyche we visited. And thys Day we retornyd to Bethphage, ffrom thens our Savyr Crist Sent ij Discipulis to Jherusalem, vpon palmys sonnday, ffor an asse, seying, Ite in Castellum qd contra vos est.

Thanne we made an ende of all our pylgrymags, And retornyd to Mownte Syon to Dyner, wher we had a ryght honeste Dyner of the wardens Costes, And at myddys of the Dyner he mad a Ryght holy and a ffamous sermon vn ta vs. And restyd vs ther all that Day.

And as we went to Bethanye, ffyrst we come to the howse of Judas, And a for hys Doore ys the place wher he hanged hym self, et Crepuit medius.

And ther we se the Dede see perfyghly, wher the v Citees stod that Sanke for synne.

Munday, that was Septem Dormiencium,* we com wery erly in

---

* The Seven Sleepers of Ephesus, 27th July.

the mornyng to Mounte Syon, And ther we hard messe and brake ower fasts. Thanne we taryed long for our assys. And thanne ther we toke humnle our leve of the holy places, And of the most blyssyd Citee of Jherusalen. And thus with ryghth light and Joyous hertis, by warnyng of our Dragman and guydes, The same Day, at viiij of the cloke in the mornyng, We found all redy, the lordes, Turkis, and Sarrasyns, Mamolukes, as well of Jherusalem, as of Rama. And other with ther folkes, to a grett nowmber of horsemen, to condyte vs to Jaffe. And so at the mownte Syon, we toke our assys, And Rode forthe at the seyd tyme. And be syd the Castell of Emaus we rest vs, and refresshyd vs with suche wyne and mete as we browght with vs from Jherusalem, and a bowght vj of the cloke at aftyr noon, we com to Rama, and lityd ther at the hospitall, beyng ryght wery of that Jorney, ffor the bestys that we rode vpon, ryght weke and ryght simple, and evyll trymed to Jorney with wher we lay all that nyght.

Tewysday, abowzt viij or ix of the cloke, we toke our assis and cam towardes Jaffe, the Turkes constreynyd vs to tary by the space of iiij howers, and ther we lay in the sande, and the sonne bornyng excedyngly hoote, whiche was gretly to our payne. And ther we war ryght evyll intreated by the Turkes and Sarrasyns many weys, and in grett fere, which war to long to wryte.

The same nyght, with grett Diffyculty and moche paciens, we war Delived a borde into ower Shippe.

And ther we lay at ankyr, wedynesday and thursday, all Day.

The cause was ther com many infideels and bowght many sondry thyngs in our shippe.

The fryday, the last Day of Julii, a bowght v of the cloke in the mornyng, we made sayle to warde Cypress homward with ryght grett joy and solas.

Tewysday, the iiij^th Day of August, we come to Cypres, And ther we lay at the Towne, whiche ys callyd Salyns,* by the space of iiij wekes and on Day.

And whyles we lay in Cypres, many of our pylgrymes went to see the Cityes in the Countre ther a bowght, And som visited pylgrymages.

A bowt iij myle from ffamagust ys an old Castell wherin Seynt Katherine was borne, and she was the kyngs Dowghter of that yle callyd Costus, as it is shewyd ther aswell by wrytyng as be reportt, She was martyred in the Citye of Alexandre, And born by the handys of Aungellys to the Mownte Synay, And ther buryed by the seyd Aungellys.

Also the xxv Day of August, that was Seynt Bertilmews Day, the morne aftyr Seynt Bertilmew, Decessyd Roberd Crosse, of London, Pewterer, and was buryed in the Chirche yard in Salyns. And xxvij Day of August, Decessyd Syr Thomas Toppe, a prest of the west countre, And was Cast over the borde, As was many moo whos soules god assoyle. And thanne ther Remayned in the shippe iiij Englyssh prestis moo.

---

* Salamis, near Famagusta.

Wedynsday, the **xxvj** Day of August, a bowt **x** of the cloke in the morning, we made Sayle to wardys the Rodes, Neverthelesse the wynd was soo streyneable a yens vs, that we made nott spede, but sumtyme sealyd bakward, sumtyme forward, by the Coste of Cipres. And thus fonde the wynde a gens vs or ellys such calmys that we sped but lytyll of our waye.

And aftyr that, nott in shorte tyme, we com ny the mountaynes of Turkey, in asia. And sone aftyr we passyd by Mirrea,* wher Seynt Nicholas was Bisshope.

And thus we Sayled thorow the Gulf of Seynt Elene, otherwyse callyd. the Gulf of Satalie,† And com a long the Costes of Turkey, And ther we saw the Mowntaynes of Macedonye.

And in the Gulfe aforseyd, Seynt Elyne kest on of the holy nayles in to the see to sease the tempest.

ffryday, the **xxv** Day of Septembre, we had siygte of the yle of the rodes Sonnday a for the ffeste of Seynt Michell, we come to the Rodes to Dyner, And ther myself lay seke by the space of **vj** wekys.

Off our cher and well entretyng at the rodys, And what Comfort was Don to vs, and Speciall that was seke and desesyd, by Sir Thomas Newporte, And Mayster William Weston, And Syr John Bowthe, and aftyrward by other Jentylmen of Englond ther, it war to long to wrytte.

Att the Rodes, In the Chyrche of Seynt John, ys many grett

---

* Myra.   † Perhaps Adalia.

reliques, The fynger of Seynt John, that he showyd ower savor with whanne he seyd Ecce Agnus Dei.

In the place of the lordes mysteres,* ys a fayer Chapell in the whiche Chapell ther ys on of the thornys that our lorde was corwnyd with and every good fryday from ix of the Cloke to it be x, it burgyns† and waxe grene, etc.

The morne aftyr Seynt Martyn, that was the xij Day of nomevbr, at j of the clok att aftyr noon, I toke shippyng at the Rodis, it was a shippe of the rodys, And fryday, the xiij Day nomebr, we com to an ylonde callyd Calamo, C myle from the Rodes, And it pteyneth to the Rodes. Sonnday, the xv Day of Novembre, we came to an yland callyd Meleo, vndernethe the Domynycon of the Venescians, iij (C) myle from the Rodes, in thys yle ys made grett plente of mylstonys, And brunstonys, And also grett plente of Partyrege and veri good wynes. -

The wynde being ev streyght and contrarius a gens vs, that we myght nott make no Sayle in Cristmasse wek. The same Day that was the xxviij Day of December, at ij or iij of the cloke, at myd nyght we made Sayle. Tewysday, Seynt Thomas Day, Erly in the morning, we Discoverd nott fare from vs iij grett shippys. And thanne we war in Grett fere, ffor we wende they had be Turkes, but ther war not soo. They war Cristen Men, we made to wardes them, for to have Spoke with som of them to know what Tydyngs they browgh owt of ffraunce, and Sodenly on of the shippes Shott a goone at vs, And hit ower Shippe and

---

* Masters of the order of St. John.   † Buds.

Stoke A Sonnder on of our grett Cables, god be thankyd no man was harmyd nor hurte.

Thanne he made vs to mayne, that ys to sey stryk Downe ower sayles.

The same Seynt Thomas Day the Martir, we traversed the see, And the morow aftyr. And also Newyers Day, sumtyme bakward, sumtyme forward, both Day and nyght, in gret fer be the coste of Turkey.

Satyrday, the secunday of Januarii, the wynde made well for vs in ower way.

Sunday, the wynde began to Ryse in the north, And munday all Day and all nyght it blew owtrageowsly.

Indured a wondred grett Tempest, As well by excedyng wonders blowing of wynde as by contynuall lythynyng. So that the capteyne, and the patron, And all the knyghtys of the Rode, whych war ther to the nowmbyr of viiij, wendyd we shulde a be lost.

The same nyght, a bowte x of the Cloke, we all promysyd pylgrymage to ower lady of grace of Missena in Cecylia. And every man Delivered hys offeryng the same tyme to the patrone of the shippe. Tewysday, the v Day of Januarii, we Seyleyd vp and Down in the Gulff of Venys, ffor the wynde was so straygth a yens vs that we myght not Kepte the Ryght wey in no wyse, And sore we war offeryd to be dryff in to Barbaria, where Dwellyth ower Mortall Enimys, As Turkes, Mamnoluks, Sarrazyns, and other infidelys.

Wednesday, the vj Day of Januarii, the wynde Rose a yens vs, with grett tempest, thonnderyng and lyghtnyng all Day and all nyght, So owtrageowsly, that we know not wher wee war.

And thanne we putt vs all in the Mercy of god, beyng in grett peyne and woo both Day and nyght, voowyng sum of vs pylgrylmages to our blyssyd lady of Lorett in ytalya, and sum to our lady of Walsyngham,* and sum to Seynt Thomas of Cannterbury, we that war englysshmen.

The Patrone of our Shippe garderd mony of vs for to make our offeryng to the iij kyngs of coloney,† And as sone as we cam on londe we shuld have Messe in the honor of them.

And in thys fforsayd long Contynual tempeste and storme we war Dreff bakward iij C myle.

Thursday, the vij Day of Januarii, the Maryoners made a grett Showte, seyng to vs that they sey londe. Thanne they war glade, and we also. And the same nyght we came to the Porte callyd Shefelanya,‡ vnder the Venycians, And whanne we shuld a take the Porte Sodenly fell down and Deyde the Pylate of our shippe, which we call lodysman. And thanne we had a grett lose, ffor he was a good honest person, on whose Soule Jhu have mercy.

In thys yle ys good wynes and grett Chepe, Plente of lambes,

---

* This shrine and that of Canterbury are fully described in a well known volume edited by John Gough Nichols.

† The three kings of Cologne.   ‡ Cephalonia.

Gotys, motons, and also hennys, and capons. In all thes for sayd yles ys growing wondyr myche licores, tyme, Sage, ffyggs, Oryges, Pomgarnetts, smale Reysyns, which we call Reyse of Corans.

Whanne we lay in thys yle oftyntymes we went on londe and hard messe, and in the yle callyd Shefelaria Dwellyd Hercules, thys yle ys vj C myle ffrom the Rodes.

Also a man that was born in thys yle told vs that they had no Rayne by the space of x months, they sow ther whete with owt Rayne, Croppyd them with owt Rayne, And made ther wyne with owt Rayne. In thys yle we lay xxv Days.

Sonnday, the last Day of Januarij, we made sayle to wards Missena, in Cecyll, with lesse wynd, and munday all Day.

Tewysday, the ij Day of Februarii, that was the Purificacon of our lady, the wynde made well for us.

Wedynsday, Seynt Blasies Day, the wynde Rose in the Suth-weste, so contynued all Day And all nyght, and thursday all Day and all nyght, that it put vs many tymes on Joypert of our lyff, and sped no thyng of our Ryght weye.

ffriday, the v Day of ffebruarii, proched nye the Cyte of Corfew, but the wynde enforcyd So myche and so strayte a yens vs, that our govenor Saw it was not possible for to wyne the porte of the Cite of Corfewe.

Satyrday, that was the Vedasti et Amandi,* we passyd by the

---

* Festival of SS. Vedast and Amandus, 6th February.

forseyd havyn, with grett wynde, thunderyng, and lytenyng owt of mesur, and so contynued a mervelows grett tempeste And storme, the same day, lx or lxxx myle from Corfew, we gate an haven a mong the Rokkes and monteyns, in grett parell, whiche havyn ys callyd Swafane, in Turkey, And whanne we war inne we cowd nott get owt nor kast our Anker for the grett Depes that was ther in shorte tyme.

They cowd not fynd no londe at iiij score fadom, Also the grett tempest contynowd so owtrageowsly, that we war never in such a fer in all our lyff. And at the last they kest ij grett ankers to gedyr, And as god wold they toke hold.

And thanne the Maryoners brake the ordinar takele of the shippe, the somer * Castyll Chambers, Dores, wyndows, and all maner of bordys, that the wynde myght have hys cowse att more large.

And thanne we all promyseyd pylgrymages to our blyssyd lady of Lorett, in Italee. The Maryorners seyng to vs they never see nor hard of such a wynde in all their lyffs. And it contynowed the same Satyrday tyll it was myd nyght. And in the same yle callyd Swafana, in Turkey, we a bode v days, and Dyverse knyghes of the Rodes went on londe with ther hande gonnes and slew horse for ther hawkes that war in the sheppe, ther war in the shippe j C hawkes and moo.

Thursday, the xij Day of ffebruarij, a bowte x or xj of the

---

* Meant for fower, fore, but written wrongly by the copier.

clok at night, we made Sayle bakward j C myle to wards Corfew, whyche we passyd by a fore, be cause our vitales war ner spent.

ffryday, the xij Day of ffebruarij, we cam in to the havyn of Corfewe, whiche Cite and yle ys vnder the Venycianns.

Satyrday we com on lande, yt ys a good Citie, the ys also a castyll, and a stronge stonding vpon a Roke of Stone in the see, and it ys excedeynly full of peple, and Specially of Jewys.

The same Satyrday ther Justyng and ronnyng with sperys. Also Sonnday And Munday, And was shewyd ther many Dyverse fetis of werre.

In thys Citye ther ys plente of brede and wyne, and good cher, And schase of fysshe many tymes. Ther ys also the fayerest yle of comodites than ony man may see, And the felde full of whete benys, wynes, and specially of Olyff trees, we went of on pylgrymage to our blyssyd lady, a myle from the Citye, the fayerst grounde that ever I saw in my lyff.

Satirday a for the fyrst Sonnday of clene lent, the xx Day of ffebruarii, we went in to the castell a mong the Jewys, it was ther Sabaday.

The same Day ther was a Jewe maryed, and aftyr Dyner I saw them Danse in a grett Chamber, bothe men and women, in Ryche apparell, Damaske, Saten, velvett, weryng a bowte ther nekkys chenys of fine gold with many Rynggs on ther fyngers with stonys of grett pryce, She that was Maryed, she had vpon her hede a crowne of gold. On of the Jewys be gan to syng, And than all the women Daunsed to gedyr by the space of an ower.

And aftyr that ther cam in yong men, on of them sang, Thanne the men and women Dauncyd to geder. Aftyr that they callyd in ther mynstrellys, and so the Dauncyd iij long bowrys.

They be fayer women, wonderful werkes in Sylk and gold and many goodly thyngs they have to sell in thys cetye, we a bode ther by the space of xiiij Dayes.

ffriday, the xxvj Day of ffebruaij, at iiij of cloke at aftyr none, we made Sayle towardes Myssena, Cecyll.*

Satyrday, the xxvij Day of ffebruarij, we lay xx from Corfew, for the wynde was so·a yens vs, we myght pass no father. Ther ys a wonder fayer Chapell of o͏ʳ lady, and many grett myracles ys shewyd ther, ther we bood vij Dayes.

ffryday, the v Day of Marche, at x of the cloke in the mornyng, we made Sayle with scase wynde, and pasyd Corfew ageyne, and so in to the Gulf of Venyse.

Satyrday and Sonnday the wynde made well for vs.

Munday, the viij Day of Marche, we came to Calabria, perteynyng to the kyngdom of Napolis, now vnder the kynge of Spayne. Ther we lay by cause the wynd was a yens vs. Ther ys grett plente of whete, and many strong Castylls stondyng, a wonderfull hyth Rokke of Stone, I never saw suche in all my lyff.

Also ovyr the watyr on the other syd, which ys Distant a Calabria xxiij myle, ys the yle of Cecyll in the whyche yle by

---

* Messina, Sicily.

the see syde ys Mons Ethneus* whiche brennyth both Day and nyght, ye may se the smoke come owt of the Toppe of it. Ther cam owt of thys hyll fyer ronnyng Downe like as it had be a flode of watyr in to the Citye, which stondyth by the see syd, and brent many howses, And also Shippes that war in the havyn, And put the City, whiche ys callyd Cathanea, in grett Juberte, wher the holy body of Seynt Agathe lyes, And by the myracle of the veyle of Seynt Agathe the Citee a for rehersyd was preservyd.

Thursday, the xj Day of Marche, we went on londe, in Calabria, hyred horses and mules, and rode by the space of xx and cam to a fayer towne callyd Regio, that stondyth on the watyr syde, and ther we lay all nyght.

ffryday, the Day of Seynt Gregori, we toke a barke at the forseyd Regio, and sayle over the watir to Myssena, whiche ys xij myle ov. And ther we abode v Dayes.

Thys Missena, in Cecyll, ys a fayer Cite and well wallyd wᵗ many fayer towers and Divse castell, the fayerst havyn for Shippes that ev I saw, ther ys also plente of all maner of thyngs that ys necessari for man, except clothe, that ys very Dere ther, ffor englyssh men brynge it thedyr by watyr owt of and a Enlong,† it ys a grett long wey, iij mˡ myle and iij C by watir.

And so it Dothe appere hev that we war saylyng in the see be twyx the Rodes and Cicyll xxiij wekes, and it ys but m myle.

---

* Etna.　　　　† England.

H

Wedynsday aftyr mydlent Sonday, that was the xvij Day of Marche, at vj of the clok at aftyr non, we toke a barke at the seyd Missena, And Rowe over a geyne to Calabrya, and so passyd by the shore by the space of a C myle.

SatyrDay, the xx Day of Marche, the aftyr non, we cam on londe not with stondyns evy Day of the for seyd iiij Days at non and at nyght we cam on londe.

Passion Sonnday, aftyr masse, we hyred horse and mules to the tyme we came to Napylles, And also men to Ronne by vs on fote to bryng the horse and mules a geyne.

Fryday, the xxvj Day of Marche, we cam to a fayer Citee, stondyng on the see syde, whyche ys callyd Salarno.

Satyrday a for palme Sonnday, at iiij of cloke at aftyr noon, we cam to the noble Citee of Napyllys, and thanne the same Satyrday, at nyght, we hyred new fres horses to the tyme we came to Rome.

At Napyllys, on palme sonnday, we hard Divne servyce, Also ther ys the fayerst castyll that ever I sawe, the gatys be goodly and made of whith marlle. Also with owt the Citys ys an horse wey vnder neth a mownteyn, by the space of a myle, a mervelous cave in the grounde, which we rode thorow the same palme Sonnday aftyr messe towards Rome.

Wedynsday, the last Day of Marche, a bowte v of the clok, at aftyr noon, we com to Rome, And ther we a bode Mawdleyn thursday, Good fryday, Ester evyn, Ester Day, And also Ester munday, and visityd the holy places with in the Cite and with owt.

Ester munday we bowght in Rome Ryght good horse that browght vs well in to Englande.

Ester tewysday, abowght x of the cloke, we Departyd from Rome. The wey from Rome it ys knowen perfyghthly I now with many Sondry persons ιo Englond, And ther for I Doo not wryght itt.

Wedynsday, the Ascencion evyn, the xj Day of [Apyll] we cam to Seynt John of Amyas,* ther I offerd.

ffryday aftyr we came to our lady of Boleyn,† and ther I offerd.

SatyrDay aftyr the Ascension, we com to Caleys by noon, And ther we lay all nyght, and sonnday all Day and all nyght.

The same Sonnday, at nyght, we shippyd our horses at Caleys.

And munday, that was the xvij Day of Apryll, we com to Dover, and lay ther all nyght.

Tewysday a for whith Sonnday, we cam to Canterbury, to Seynt Thomes Messe, And ther I offeryd and made an ende of my pylgrymage. Deo gracias.

Note that be thys forseyd processe wreten of thys seyd Jurney that we Departyd owt of Inglonde the xx Day of Marche, the yer of oᵲ lord God, mlccccc and xvij, and we came to Venyce the xxix

---

* Amiens.　　† Boulogne.

Day of Apryll, whyche ys v wekys an v Days, And ther we lay at Venece tyll the xiiij Day of Junii, whyche ys vj wekes and iiij Dayes.

The xij Day of Julii, we cam to Jaff, and so spendyd owtwardes be twyne Venyce and Jaffe on moneth and ij Dayes, And her we lay in the same Porte iij Days.

Also we taryed in the holy londe vnto the xxix day of Julii, whiche Day we retornyd to ower shippe. And so it appereth hat we war in the holy londe xv Dayes.

The xij Day of Marche, we com to Missena, In Cecyll, And the xv Day of Apryll we com to Calys.

And the xvij Day of Apryll we come to Dover, And so we war owt of Enlong in ower seyd Pylgrymage the space of an holl yer v wekys and iij Dayes.

By the accompte a forseyd that it shewyth it ys

ffrom Venyce to Parence, C myle.
ffrom Parens to Jarra, C mble.
ffrom Jarra to Lesena, C myle li.
ffrom Lesena to Araguse, CC myle.
ffrom Araguse to Corfew, CCC myle.
ffrom Corfew to Modona, CCC myle.
ffrom Modona to Candia, CCC myle.
ffrom Candia to Rodys, CCC myle.
ffrom the Rodes to Cipres, CCCC myle,
ffrom Cipres to Jaff, CCCC myle.

ffrom Jaff to Jherusalem, XL myle.

Sm xxvj C myles.

ffrom Englond to Venice, vij C myle.

ffrom Englond to Jherusalem, iij m^l myle and iij C.

Of the Temple of Salomon.

Whyle we war thus occupyd in our pylyrymage at Jherusalem And ther a bowyt, we passyd Sundry tymes by the temple of Salomon, and often we Sawe it and behelde it with owt forth ffrom Sundry hylls, and specially from the Mownte of Olivete, ffor ther ys the most clere sight and best beholdyng ther of to them that may not entre in to it. And be twyne the Temple of Salomon and the Mownte of Olivete ys the vale of Josophat. The Sarrasyns woll sofer no Cristen men to com with in the seyd Temple.

And yf he Doo he shalbe compellyd incontynently to for sake hys fayth and Cristendom or ellys to be put to execucion of Dethe by and bye.

Ther ys also with in the circuyte of the walles of the same, an other Temple that was callyd Porticus Salomonis, whiche ys also wonder grett and large, And it ys sayd ther be continually brennyng, with in Salomons Temple vij C lampes, And in porticu Salamonis viij C lampys.

Thys Temple hath Sundry gatts to entre in to it, the iij gatts with in the citye, whiche I saw all iij, An other gate ys with owt forth Estwarde toward the Mounnte of Olivete, that ys callyd the goldyn gate. In at the same gate Rode ower blyssyd Savyor upon palme Sonday, Sittyng vpon the Asse.

But as I sayd befor ther ys no Cristen man sufferyd to com ny it, but what so ev pylgryme loke Devowtly to wardys the same gate and be hold it with Devocion hath grauntyd to hym plenarye Remission.

The Sarrasyns have thys Temple in gret reverence, and specially they worshippe ther a Rokk of Stone, whyche ys closyd a bowte with Irron, And they Rekyn it so holy that no Sarrasyn Dare towche it. How be it they com from p-ties to visit it.

In the same Rook with in the sayd Temple, the Jewes kepe the Arke of god, with the reliques that Titus caryed from Rome, that ys to sey the x commaundments, Arons rodde, Moyes Roode, A vessell of gold, full of Mauna, Ornamentis for Sacryfyce, the Tabernacle of Aron, a sqware table of gold with xij precious Stonys, a box with grene Jaspys with iiij fyngerys, conteynyng the viij names of ower lorde, vij candylstykkys of golde, and An Auter of fyne gold, upon the whyche they have a cherybyn of gold xij spane longe, And a Tabernacle of golde and xij Trumpetts of sylv, A Tabernacle of Sylver and vij barley lovys, And all the other reliques that war be for the Nativite of Criste.

Up on the same Rokk sleppe Jacobbe whanne he sawe Aungellys goo vp and Down, And sayd, Vere locus iste Sanctvs est et ego nesciebam. And ther the Aungell changyd Jacobs name and callyd hym Israel.

Item, our Savyor Criste was offeryd vyon the same stone whanne

Symeon Justus toke hym in hys Armys and sayd, Nunc Dimittis svum tuum.

Item, or Savyor Criste sat vp on the same Rokke at xij yer of Age, in the myddys of the Doctors heryng them and opposyng them.

And aftyr wardys at hys xxx yer of age, many tymes he satt vpon the same prechyng to the peple, And ther ower Savyor Criste for gaff the woman hyr synnys that was taken in Avoutry.

And ther offeryd fyrst Melchesedech bred and wyne to ower lord in token of the sacrament that was for to com.

And ther the Aungell Denowncyd to Zacharie the Nativite of Seynt John the Baptyst.

Item, ther fell David praeying to our lord for mercy for hym self and hys peple.

And with in the same Temple ys the ffountayne wher of holy wrytt seyte, Vidi aquam egredientem de templo.

The iiij gate of thys Temple ys with owt the Citye, Suthest towards the Mownte Syon, And that ys callyd Porticus Salomonis, with in the whyche gate ther ys a fayer Chirche and a large of our blyssyd lady wher she was Noryshed and browght vp to the tyme she was xiiij yer of Age.

Holy scriptur spekyth moche of thys Temple whiche war to longe to wryte for this purpose.

Tempus Deviacionis fuit ab Adam usque ad Moysen quia tunc

deviabant per ydolatriam.   Tempus renovacionis a Moyse usque ad Xpi nativitatem Tempus regressionis sive recosiliacionis est a nativite Xpi usque ad assenciorem.   Tempus peregrinacionis ab assencione Xpi usque ad finem mundi.   Tempus Deviacionis representat Ecclesiam in lxx un de tunc legitur, Penthateuchum et fit memoria De miseria hominis vel ade cum dictum est.   In Sudore vultus tui.

y^e Leadenhalle Presse, E.C.

Amongst the Shans. By Archibald Ross Colquhoun, A.M.I.C.E., F.R.G.S., Author of "Across Chrysê." With upwards of Fifty whole-page Illustrations. Edited by Holt S. Hallett, M.I.C.E., F.R.G.S. [*Nearly ready.* 21s.

FIELD & TUER, Ye Leadenhalle Presse, E.C.

The Pyramids and Temples of Gizeh. By W. M. Flinders Petrie. Containing an account of excavations and surveys carried on at Gizeh during 1880-1-2; with the application of the results to various modern theories of the pyramids. [*Just published, crown 4to, 250 pp. and* 17 *plates, price* 18s.

FIELD & TUER, Ye Leadenhalle Presse, E.C. -

An Essay of Scarabs. By W. J. Loftie,
B.A., F.S.A. (Author of " A History of London.")
Together with a Catalogue of Ancient Egyptian
Amulets of various kinds, bearing the names of
Kings. [*In preparation.*

FIELD & TUER, Ye Leadenhalle Presse, E.C.

Collectors' Marks. By Louis Fagan,
with Frontispiece by the Author. (For the use
of Print Collectors.) [*Just out.* 21S.

FIELD & TUER, Ye Leadenhalle Presse, E.C.

Crawhall's Chap-book Chaplets:
Adorn'd with suitable Sculptures. *The many
hundreds of cuts being all hand-coloured, the
issue is necessarily limited.* Contents of the
Volume : I. The Barkshire Lady's Garland.
II. The Babes in the Wood. III. I know what I
know. IV. Jemmy and Nancy of Yarmouth.
V. The Taming of a Shrew. VI. Blew-cap for
me. VII. John and Joan. VIII. George
Barnewel. [*Now ready. In one thick 4to vol.,* 25s.

FIELD & TUER, Ye Leadenhalle Presse, E.C.

Olde ffrendes wyth newe Faces:

Adorn'd with suitable Sculptures. *The many hundreds of cuts being all hand-coloured, the issue is necessarily limited.* Table of the Matter herein contained : I. The louing Ballad of Lord Bateman. II. A true relation of the Apparition of Mrs. Veal. III. The Long Pack : A Northumbrian Tale. IV. The Sword Dancers. V. John Cunningham, the Pastoral Poet. VI. Ducks and Green Peas, or the Newcastle Rider : a Tale in Rhyme. VII. Ducks and Green Peas : a Farce. VIII. Andrew Robinson Stoney Bowes, Esquire. IX. The Gloamin' Buchte.
[*In preparation. In one thick* 4*to vol.,* 25*s.*
Field & Tuer, Ye Leadenhalle Presse, E.C.

Prince Pertinax :

A Fairy Tale, by Mrs. George Hooper, Authoress of " The House of Raby," " Artell," &c. Illustrated with Twenty-six drawings in sepia by Margaret L. Hooper and Margery May. *A charming present.* [*Now ready.* 21*s.*
Field & Tuer, Ye Leadenhalle Presse, E.C.

London Cries : With **Six Charming Children** and about Forty other Illustrations; the text by Andrew W. Tuer.

[*In the press.* 21*s.*

FIELD & TUER, Ye Leadenhalle Presse, E.C.

When is your Birthday? or a Year of Good Wishes. Set of Twelve Designs by Edwin J. Ellis, with Sonnets by the Artist. *A beautiful book.* [*Now ready.* 21*s.*

FIELD & TUER, Ye Leadenhalle Presse, E.C.

Journals and Journalism : With a Guide for Literary Beginners. By John Oldcastle. Beautifully bound in vellum, old style. Contents : Literary Amateurs. Introduction to Editors. How to begin. "Declined with thanks." Literary Copyright. Pounds, Shillings, and Pence. Journalism as a Career. In an Editor's Chair. Ten Journalistic Commandments. How to Correct Proofs; and a Directory of the Periodical Press, being a list of Journals and Magazines, the Address of their Offices, the Names of their Editors, and a Sketch of their History and Scope. [*Price 3s. 6d.*

· FIELD & TUER, Ye Leadenhalle Presse, E.C.

Bartolozzi and his Works:

(Dedicated by permission to Her Majesty the Queen), Biographical, Anecdotal and Descriptive. By Andrew W. Tuer. Beautifully illustrated with engravings in red and brown of the St. James' and St. Giles' Beauties, from the original copperplates engraved by Bartolozzi in 1783, &c., &c. In two handsome vellum-bound 4to volumes. [*Price £3 3s.*

"We can sincerely praise the labour and taste that have produced this beautiful book."—*Daily News*.

"Contains a wealth of information."—*Times*.

"A masterpiece."—*Magazine of Art*

FIELD & TUER, Ye Leadenhalle Presse, E.C.

Glass in the Old World: By M. A.

Wallace-Dunlop, With Illustrations. "By far the most comprehensive, comprehensible, complete, and at the same time entertaining book on old glass that has yet been published in English."—*Saturday Review*. [*Price 12s. 6d.*

FIELD & TUER, Ye Leadenhalle Presse, E.C.

The Marriage Ring ; or the Mysteri-
ousness and Duties of Marriage. By Dr. Jeremy
Taylor, with an Introduction by the Rev. J. A.
Kerr. [*Price 2s. 6d.*

FIELD & TUER, Ye Leadenhalle Presse, E.C.

Secrets of the Sanctum : An Inside
View of an Editor's Life. Only a few copies
left. [*Price 6s.*

FIELD & TUER, Ye Leadenhalle Presse, E.C.

Book of Japanese Designs, about
350 in all, many being very intricate and beautiful, and of a character most useful to artist-
designers. A few copies only. [*Price 3s. 6d.*

BYGONE BEAUTIES:

"A SELECT SERIES OF POR-
TRAITS OF LADIES OF RANK
AND FASHION," painted by
john Hoppner, R.A., and engraved by Charles Wilkin;
with notes by Andrew W.
Tuer.

[*In the Press.* 21*s.*

FIELD & TUER, Ye Leadenhalle Presse, E.C.

Lightning Source UK Ltd.
Milton Keynes UK
UKHW050636120922
408721UK00006B/635

9 781249 51232